GAMBLING: NEVADA STYLE

GAMBLING:
Nevada Style

MAURICE LEMMEL

DOLPHIN BOOKS
Doubleday & Company, Inc.
Garden City, N.Y.
1966

This book is dedicated to my wife
JOSEFINA
and my daughters
AÏDA *and* NANCY

Gambling: Nevada Style was originally published in hardcovers by Doubleday & Company, Inc., in 1964. The Dolphin Books edition is published by arrangement with Doubleday & Company, Inc.

Dolphin Books edition: 1966

The best place to get information about Nevada gambling is right in the casinos themselves. Yet even this approach, if you depend entirely on others to supply that information, can be frustrating.

You may have been led to believe that gambling-casino dealers will be happy to answer any of your questions. I found that you don't always get the right answers, frequently you get none at all, and some dealers aren't happy when you ask them questions that test what they should know about their own work.

So I started from scratch and personally learned all I could about the five games described in this book by watching how they were conducted, playing them myself, and questioning hundreds of players and casino employees.

I discovered that there are significant regional differences in Nevada gambling. Keno tickets in southern Nevada vary in important details from those in northern Nevada. Craps in Las Vegas is not the same as Craps in Reno. In the "21," or Blackjack, game there are so many different ways of handling the various features that you may find it conducted differently in every casino you visit.

After having gathered the information for what I believed would be a better book on Nevada gambling, I made a survey of the need for such a book. Responsible professional gambling people advised me that they welcomed a correct description of their games by an outsider not connected with gambling through ownership or employment. I did not intend to identify any of the casinos or any individuals who had a direct interest in gambling.

This purely objective, noncommercial treatment of gambling operations gave me the freedom to criticize anything I didn't like. In addition to the criticisms I make in this book, I bring out some of the best features of Nevada gambling which have received little or no publicity, such as Faro and the Crap tables with 10-cent or 25-cent minimum bets in downtown Las Vegas and Reno.

Gambling is not a static subject. Many changes took place during 1964, Nevada's centennial year. This book was the first book on gambling to take notice of them. Changes made since the publication of *Gambling: Nevada Style* in the original hardcover edition are incorporated in this paperback edition.

Changes made during the spring of 1964 in the playing rules for Blackjack in the Las Vegas casinos placed some speculation on the future of that game there. The old rules were quickly reinstated when Las Vegas found, as I had already correctly predicted, that it would gain nothing by the tighter Blackjack rules briefly in effect.

The familiar silver dollar disappeared from the Nevada gambling tables in 1964, and $1 chips, or *checks* as they are correctly referred to in the gambling business, replaced the "hard money." Legislation effective in 1965 authorized the use of dollar-size metal tokens which would work in $1 slot machines and electronic Blackjack machines.

I point out that the state supervision and the highly competitive status of legal gambling in Nevada are factors that make the gambling games in Nevada superior, from the player's point of view, to those same games played elsewhere.

Some interesting facts about the five most important Nevada casino games are divulged here for the first time. This book contains the first accurate mathematical breakdown for all straight Keno tickets from one up to fifteen spots, with the correct probabilities and house percentages given.

My appreciation is extended to the office of the Governor and to the two State of Nevada agencies which regulate and have authority over the legal gambling business—the Gaming Commission and the Gaming Control Board—for the information and statistics they have provided me.

I also wish to thank the many helpful gambling professionals who have enabled me to portray the Nevada casino games as they are actually conducted. This acknowledgment to casino managements and employees is of course made in the aggregate rather than individually.

M. L.

CONTENTS

My first adventure with legal gambling in Nevada was a memorable one, if only for its short duration. I went broke in exactly four throws of the dice.

I had been in Nevada many times previously for the winter sports, and although I had passed by the gambling casinos in Reno or at Lake Tahoe on those trips, it never occurred to me that someday I would find in the galloping dominoes or the Roulette wheel a substitute for the more strenuous outdoor sports.

My introduction to legal gambling was accidental. On one of my winter sports excursions in the late 1930s my return was delayed until snowplows could clear the roads of the drifts accumulated by a blizzard still in progress. I had $20 in cash with me, and with nothing more important to do than kill time, I followed the crowd into one of the downtown Reno gambling casinos.

I knew practically nothing about any of the games, but I remembered reading somewhere that the Don't Pass bet in Craps has the least percentage in favor of the house. I decided to play it that way and wandered over to a Crap table to test my luck. It was positively rotten.

Five dollars of my money went on the Don't Pass line just as an attractive brunette who had begun shooting the dice threw a seven. I lost. Once more I bet against the dice, and again she threw a seven. Well, she can't do it all the time, I thought, so I repeated my bet, and for the third time in a row seven came up. It happened again for the fourth time. In less time than it took you to read this paragraph, my bankroll went from $20 down to zero.

Although I couldn't prove anything, I had a strong suspicion that I was the victim of "dirty work" on the part of the casino or some of its employees. The possibility of that was fresh on my mind because the few books available on gambling that I had read emphasized the many ways in which a gambler can be cheated by the use of crooked dice or rigged equipment.

Later on in the same year I was not far from Reno on a deer-hunting trip. Boca Mountain, northeast of Truckee, California, annually produces a kill of about 120 legal bucks on the opening day of the deer season. This area is popular with sportsmen because the hunting can be combined with fishing in the many nearby lakes and streams.

While the deer-hunting effort collectively seems to be good, from the standpoint of the individual hunter it is not. Divide that 120-deer kill into an estimated 6000 hunters in the field and you'll see that only one hunter in fifty will be successful. As one of the 98 percent who had no luck on opening day, I at least enjoyed the consolation of knowing that I had lots of company.

Lake Tahoe, Donner Lake, and many of the smaller bodies of water in the Sierra Nevada are the homes of trout properly classified as "tackle busters." Believe it or not, the equipment most favored not so many years ago was heavy surfcasting tackle, the kind you would use for striped-bass fishing on the ocean shore. You baited a large-sized hook with a minnow, heaved it out from the rim of the lake with a four-ounce pyramid sinker to help you, and sat and waited for a strike. It could hardly be called sport, but it did get results; trout from three to twelve pounds and sometimes heavier could be expected. The use of natural fish as bait has since been outlawed or restricted in many of these waters. Introduction of spinning tackle has completely revolutionized fishing, increasing the angler's pleasure when he makes a catch on very light tackle and, I presume, making it less disagreeable to the fish to be caught that way.

On this occasion we had neither the heavy tackle nor the minnows considered essential to any fishing success, so after a fruitless morning deer hunt I decided to hitchhike to Reno just to see what the city looked like in the daytime.

There were no freeways then and all traffic slowed to a crawl in going through Truckee's one main street. I had little difficulty getting a lift. I had plenty of time but little cash and arrived in Reno with only $2 in my pockets.

After looking over the city's major points of interest that make it an attractive community in its own right, I visited one of the gambling casinos.

Still stung by my previous fiasco at the Crap tables and the feeling that there might have been more to it than only bad luck, I tried Roulette this time. Roulette is considered to be more "honest" than any of the card or dice games because the players are not allowed to touch either the wheel or the ball. Many gamblers prefer Roulette for this reason. I was one of them.

I paid my $2 for a stack of twenty chips. I made a few wins on the even-money combinations for some fair but not spectacular success in the beginning; then I switched over to betting on single numbers and, with better-than-average luck, my capital mounted up to about $10. At this point I hit a plateau, as a statistician would describe it, where my bankroll remained about the same for a long time with not much fluctuation above or below that amount.

My betting on single numbers began with one, then two, three, and up to five chips. Finally at the 50-cent or five-chip level I hit the good luck which all gamblers hope will come their way. I was betting on 00 (double zero) and my number came up twice in about a dozen spins.

Now ahead of the gambling business for the first time in my life, I wanted to quit right there and started counting what I had on hand. I told the croupier that I would cash in my chips.

My counting was interrupted by the croupier, who

shoved $17.50—this time in silver—toward me over my pro-
tests that it wasn't my money. It took some explaining to
make me understand that by not removing my last five-
chip bet on 00, which won, this bet was still up and the
number had repeated. This came as a most pleasant surprise because in my preoccupation with counting my chips
I had not been paying attention to the wheel at all.

This time I took off the bet. In addition to the bonanza
I had stumbled into, I already had most of the chips of the
color I played with, and a few silver dollars in my pockets
from cashing in some of my chips earlier. Loaded with all
this, I retired to a Blackjack table not being used and
dumped all my wealth upon it to begin counting all over
again. I grouped the chips and coins in neat stacks and
put the count down on a piece of paper as I went along.
I planned to add the figures later, and at the moment was
satisfied that the total would be over $50.

Suddenly I realized that I had lost all track of the time
and it was already long past sunset. Rather than risk the
uncertainty of hitchhiking at night, I decided to stay overnight in Reno. I had money. I could have taken a train or
a bus to Truckee. Why didn't I? I don't know.

I strolled through the downtown section of the city,
window-shopping as I went along, and it took me almost
an hour to reach a motel in the southern section of town
where I had been before, and where I hoped to find a room
available at a reasonable price. As I was about to enter
the office, I discovered that I had no money with me!

All I had was the piece of paper with my figures on it.
The cash those figures represented was still on the Blackjack table where I had been counting it—that is, if someone else hadn't helped himself to it in the meantime.

Hurrying back to the casino to find out what happened
to my money, I had slim hopes of ever seeing it again.

It was at least an hour since I had left the casino, but to
my surprise and utter delight every bit of my change was
still exactly as I had left it, in spite of the fact that dozens

of people were walking past within arm's reach of it every minute and any one of them could have scooped up all or part of it.

One thing you can say about gambling is that there's never a dull moment. Sometimes the excitement may be more intense than at other times, but even at a minimum level it's pretty high.

What you have read up to this point clears the way for a lot of the more serious things you will have explained to you in greater detail in the pages that follow.

You'll be told that gambling as it is conducted in Nevada, when you thoroughly understand it, is a form of recreation in which you can get the greatest satisfaction and entertainment from your personal participation. That Olympic Games psychology for amateur athletes—it's not whether you win or lose that counts, but how well you play the game—can be applied to gambling also. It *is* entertainment and, when done within your means, it can give you more fun and suspense for your money than any other recreation.

In this book you'll learn that with bad gambling management and only a small amount of bad luck you'll go broke. With better management and admittedly better luck it's possible to start on a shoestring and build up a nest egg many times the value of your original capital.

You'll see that the average amateur gambler, like myself, makes his first gambling attempt without much knowledge of the mathematics or the conduct of the games he's playing and with some reasonable suspicions about the honesty of the casino and its employees and equipment. The reasons for some of these suspicions will be explained.

You'll also learn that gamblers are rather careless in the way they handle their money and can lose it in many ways other than by making the wrong guesses on their betting.

Gambling, like trout fishing in the lakes of the Sierra Nevada, has gone through a revolution in the tackle and bait that is used. I'll show you how to nibble on some of the bait without getting caught.

Just how absorbing gambling can be is best illustrated by a recent incident. It was the revelation by a professional pickpocket, now serving time in California for other crimes, that he never had to work for a living like the rest of us time-card punchers. He disclosed that he made as much as $84,000 in one year by deftly going over the patrons of Reno gambling casinos for the easy pickings there.

People are generally very careful about how they handle their money and will guard against any possible losses through theft or mishandling, but the thorough hold that gambling has on their attention makes them lose that caution.

A woman concentrating all her attention on playing two slot machines at the same time, leaving her open purse beside her, is an easy pigeon for any larcenous person who happens to be in the neighborhood. So is the man who flashes a lot of money around, then places it in a billfold which half protrudes from a pants or coat pocket.

The gambling business, and Reno in particular, were very much embarrassed about the pickpocket's disclosures, but they are not unique. Pickpockets will be attracted to anyplace where people congregate and where there is money available. The gambling casinos are doing everything in their power to combat activity of this type. The uniformed guards and the plain-clothes detectives employed by the casinos are as much for your protection as their employer's. Without further emphasis on this item, let it be a warning to the average gambler that he has much to learn about taking care of his own money.

In deciding to write a book about Craps and some of the other games of chance in Nevada, I was motivated by a number of reasons. One is that no author had ever accentuated the positive on this subject. The few books by other authors then available in bookstores and libraries were almost all written by professional magicians and sleight-of-hand artists whose interest lies in the exposure of crooked gambling equipment and methods. This information is *must* reading for casino employees, who are expected to be able to recognize a pair of crooked dice as readily as a bank teller notices counterfeit currency. However, it is doubtful that these books have been of much help to the average amateur gambler playing in Nevada, where the games are presumed to be honestly conducted and subject to the most rigid inspection.

I found the gambling public being misinformed by the very people upon whom it relies for correct information. College professors who are recognized experts at gambling odds were making serious mathematical blunders, besides exhibiting an ignorance of the games as they are actually conducted. Certain bets were being misrepresented to the players by gambling-casino employees, and I found casino managements themselves not too well acquainted with some of the mathematics of their own games.

It comes as no surprise that the customer who is doing the gambling is woefully weak in mathematical knowledge and abstract thinking, or he wouldn't be gambling at all or making some of the bets that he does.

My own serious interest in gambling was originally purely mathematical. I wanted to know the individual player's chances of success in the various games and betting options. I couldn't find all of the information I really wanted in books on gambling, and the people employed in the business couldn't supply it, so I had to work on my own to find out what it was they didn't know or were afraid to tell me. I found out plenty.

In showing you how to play Craps as it is done in Nevada, I believe I am presenting this subject completely and accurately to the American public for the first time. Most authors on gambling describe the illegal games conducted elsewhere and seem to have ignored gambling where it is done legally. In all the differences between legal and illegal gambling, the legal games will be shown to be far superior from the player's point of view.

My knowledge of gambling and particularly of Craps goes far beyond my personal experiences at the gambling tables. My statistical studies on Craps included one project of throwing over one million consecutive decisions of the dice, which would be equal to an individual gambler's playing forty hours a week for over six years at the rate of eighty decisions per hour of playing. This project enabled me to make some very significant original observations on the behavior of the dice and how I think the game should be played to the player's best advantage and enjoyment.

In comparing Craps to some of the other games having similar house percentages, I bring you for the first time a full and correct description of the Faro game. Not very much is really known about Keno, either inside or outside of the gambling business, and my analysis of this game shows that both players and gambling casinos can benefit by a few much-needed improvements in the way the game is handled financially.

Very little has ever been written about some of the other interesting aspects of legal gambling. For example, the transportation bargains made possible by some of the casinos in their competition to bring you to their doors, and the fabulous food at reasonable prices that makes any Nevada casino a gourmet's paradise. The nongambler as well as the gambler can take advantage of these "fringe benefits." Whether you gamble or not, and whatever your personal reasons may be for or against it, I feel that a knowledge of this information will add increased pleasure to your next visit to Nevada and the Far West and will save you some money too—certainly more than the price of this book.

What you read about gambling in newspapers may give you a false impression, because what makes news in gambling, as in everything else, is the mention of large sums of money. A high-rolling gambler's alleged winning of thousands of dollars forms the basis for many of these stories. Any advertisement of gambling as such or any invitation to gamble in Nevada is illegal outside that state, so the gambling casinos have to keep their names before the public by stressing the show-business talent featured at their establishments. The weekly salaries that run into four or five figures paid to entertainment headliners have to be met out of what the casinos earn from their gambling operations. This all makes Nevada gambling seem expensive and only a rich man's diversion.

It is not necessarily so, and you can play Craps in downtown Reno and Las Vegas for an average cost of less than 10 cents an hour.

In the Faro game it is possible to gamble on exactly even terms with the casino. Then your cost for gambling is absolutely nothing. Faro is vitally important to Nevada gambling because it's the best rebuttal to the criticism frequently made that a gambler can't get an even break for his money. It's available if you want it, and I'm glad to acquaint you with the game and how to play it.

"Systems" come in for discussion in most gambling literature. I don't regard them as a substitute for good luck, which you must have in your gambling, with or without a system, to make a profit from it. A good system makes your playing more enjoyable. It takes away any fears that crooked dice can be worked to your disadvantage in a Crap game. You make your bets according to a prearranged plan and, if you happen to be making too many losing bets, there's a safety factor that keeps your losses from getting out of hand. Finally, with a good system you can win just as much from what is regarded as ordinary performance of the dice as when they are continually passing or not passing. Gambling casinos have been taken for small fortunes on occasions when unusual runs of consecutive passes have been made and big-money bettors have followed their hunches with winning Pass, Come, and place bets. Your belief that with your system you can win anytime without waiting for the dice to get "hot" probably won't worry any casino management, which is always willing to accept your business, but it should put that little extra punch into your effort.

CHAPTER 1

THE PEOPLE WHO SERVE YOU

The people you do business with in Nevada casinos, especially the employees who conduct the various games you play, form a very interesting and vital part of the whole gambling picture.

How honest are they? How competent are they? How much are they paid? Do they depend on tips or other extra income? How do their earnings and working conditions compare with those of workers in nongambling services where similar skill and financial responsibility are involved? How do you go about trying to get a job in a gambling casino if you want one? These and many other questions are on the minds of all Nevada visitors.

The public hears very little about the problems of casino management and labor—problems with each other and with the people they serve. The business itself has never gone to Washington, tin cup in hand, begging for financial subsidies or any other guarantees or government aid, as have so many other sections of our national economy.

No casino has ever been closed due to a strike by employees demanding higher wages or better working conditions. Until recently there were no labor unions representing the employees who work at the gambling tables. Although I'm a supporter of organized labor myself, I have to admit that absence of employee unions in the legal gambling situation is probably a good thing for all concerned. Strict regulations are imposed by the State of Nevada as to who can or can't have a financial interest in a legal gambling casino. Individuals who make their living in the business have so far been successful in preventing any state control over their occupations.

It is not likely that individual dice and card dealers, Roulette croupiers, Keno-game employees, and others, even though not organized, will surrender control of their jobs to a labor union which they might regard as a greater threat to themselves than any governmental authority. Gangsters, hoodlums, and those with police records or undesirable personal histories, barred from ownership or employment in Nevada gambling, could sneak in through the back door with more power than ever to rule or ruin the business if they came in as officials of a powerful employees' labor union.

Tolerance of legal gambling in Nevada is based on the premise that the games will be conducted honestly, that they will provide useful tax revenue to the state and its various political subdivisions, and that undesirable elements will be kept out.

These qualifications have been substantially kept, and there is increasing likelihood that this situation will continue because gambling has now become Nevada's best single source of tax income. Any deviation from this policy could prove disastrous to the state's financial structure. The record is not 100 percent perfect, however; a lot of accusations now being made by critics of gambling could, if they were supported by adequate proof, cause a demand for abolition of legal gambling at either a statewide or national level. The Nevada State Legislature or the Congress of the United States has, in the final analysis, the real power of life and death over Nevada gambling.

If one could prove beyond a doubt that any Nevada gambling casino has ever knowingly cheated a customer through the use of crooked equipment or methods, the reaction would be swift and final. The casino would lose its license. This has already happened in the case of several casinos whose employees were caught cheating at Blackjack. A Las Vegas casino which was found by an inspector to have some irregular dice in its dice box at a Crap table was promptly put out of business. The dice weren't in use, but merely having them there was sufficient grounds for suspicion. Another Las Vegas casino lost its license to operate by being involved in an argument with a player and refusing to redeem all of the player's chips for the cash they represented.

The 42 major Nevada casinos have in excess of $140,-000,000 invested in their total operations, of which the gambling games form only a part but carry the load for the whole, just as a college or university often depends on profits from football to finance its entire athletic program. Deviation from their ideal of absolute honesty toward the customers can be considered nonexistent; they have too much to lose and it isn't worth the risk to try to cheat you. The casinos that lost their licenses were all relatively small ones.

In the beginning and for a long time afterward I had some serious personal doubts about the honesty of Nevada gambling. There are many reasons for such doubts. Some of the books which you may have already read about gambling were written with a desire to expose crooked gambling equipment and practices which existed in illegal games conducted in other states. Such equipment has been found to exist in Nevada, too, in isolated instances. When the Nevada State Gaming Control Board hired an outside expert to make a survey of the honesty of the games, he reported that Nevada gambling was 98 percent honest. The dishonesty referred to was in connection with the game of Blackjack.

Craps has been described in popular literature as the crookedest gambling game of them all, but in Craps the legal casino is much more likely to be cheated by a crooked customer than the other way around.

The average person, unable to distinguish between legal and illegal gambling, presumes that gambling in Nevada is no different than elsewhere.

Motion pictures all depict the worst features of nineteenth-century gambling. Many of the Westerns which are popular as TV serials include gambling scenes. Our hero steps into a saloon or gambling hall, puts all his money down on one big bet, loses, and then accuses the house or the dealer of being crooked. The inevitable gunplay or fistfight ensues, followed by a free-for-all which leaves the place a complete shambles. As it must be under the Hollywood code, our hero and the supporters of law and order emerge victorious.

It is rarely explained in what way the gambling was considered to be crooked or what evidence, if any, was available to back up such an accusation. About the only clear thing you're able to figure out for yourself is that if you gamble you're likely to be cheated.

News stories frequently appear about bridge-toll collectors, bus drivers, or collectors of parking meter coins who have been caught dipping their fingers into the till. You know that gambling-casino employees sometimes handle money under conditions where the exact amount in their custody can't be accurately determined, yet you never hear about any of them being tried in criminal courts or even being discharged from their jobs for financial irregularities.

The conditions under which gambling-casino employees are allowed to handle cash are the strictest of any business, with the possible exception of the United States Mint. The mirrors that you see on the walls or ceilings in most of the casinos are not ordinary ones. They're a special type, and someone behind the reflecting surface can look through them as if they were panes of ordinary plate glass. Some of the larger casinos are protected by closed-circuit television in which a monitor can observe all of the gambling games, the cashiers' cages, and the entrances and exits to the casino. Uniformed guards with miniature walkie-talkie radio sets are in constant communication with the monitor, who can alert them to anything that might be considered suspicious. Plain-clothes detectives circulate among the crowds.

The employees themselves must follow working rules which are a lot stricter than those imposed in other business activities where money is handled. Female employees can't have purses with them or wear clothes with large pockets. If it is necessary for any employees to put their hands in their pockets for any reason, it must be done in a certain approved manner. The hands must be exhibited, fingers outstretched with palms upward, to show that nothing is concealed in them. If a handkerchief is withdrawn from a pocket it has to be dangled by one corner to show that nothing is being removed or replaced other than the handkerchief. There are other checks on an employee's honesty which I'm not at liberty to describe here because such measures must be kept secret in order to be effective. You may be sure that when the employee who periodically cleans out the coins from the slot machines is making his rounds he's being watched and he knows it. Other employees are also subject to the same constant surveillance.

Nevada gambling-casino employees are fingerprinted and given a routine Police Department checkup which they must pass before they're put to work. While your own risk as to an employee's honesty is only a small one, the casino's is a lot larger and you may rest assured that if the casino management was satisfied with an employee's record and references, and hired him, he's considered above personal temptation.

In spite of this assurance, the gambling operations take place under conditions that would normally tax your unquestioned faith in the employees. You get no receipts when you lose; nor do you get an itemized written account of how much is due you on the payoff when you win.

I've observed plenty of errors being made by employees, both in regard to my own playing and while I was engaged in carrying out certain statistical projects at the gambling tables. At first these errors appear to be due to dishonesty, but on closer examination turn out to be the ordinary ones of counting or doing subtraction, multiplication, and division. They occur anyplace where money changes hands. All calculations at the gambling tables are done mentally, with no cash registers or adding machines to help the employees.

Frequently an employee will be overworked in relation to the number of persons being served. Where there are a dozen or more players at a Crap table it takes three employees to give good service. One is a stick man, who watches the dice and calls the score on each throw and the decision at the end of the roll. The other two are dealers, who each work half of the table and handle the money according to the performance of the dice and the bets being made. When an unassisted stick man is carrying the load by himself and doing all the work, it places that employee under terrific pressure. He'll rush through the payoffs with amazing speed, at some expense to accuracy.

If you don't get paid off what you think you should have received, the proper thing to do is to ask, "Is this right?" and have the employee paying you go over the transaction slowly to explain how he arrived at the amount. If he finds he made an unintentional error he'll gladly correct it with appropriate apologies. Sometimes you'll receive *more* than you should; it is not rare to find yourself getting $11 where you should have received only $10. These random errors don't worry the casino because they all tend to even themselves out and in the long run will be nullified, but to the individual player they are important.

What you might regard as being shortchanged can take place when you're served by an employee whose training or previous experience has been at tables with layouts different from the one at which you're playing. If the dealer previously worked in a casino that pays 30 *for* 1 and he's now working where the payoff is 30 *to* 1 on a proposition bet, he could, under pressure of the action at the moment and without thinking, pay you a dollar less than you should receive. A 30 *to* 1 payoff gives you back $31 on a $1 bet;

you get back your dollar plus the $30 you won from the house. It's up to the customer to be alert for errors.

Another possible area for errors involves the barred number on the come-out for Don't Come or Don't Pass bets where it's a stand-off instead of a loss to the house. In Las Vegas the barred number on all the layouts I have seen is 12. In northern Nevada there is a preference toward using 2 as the barred number. Many of the veteran Las Vegas dealers work at Lake Tahoe during the summer vacation season. What is a stand-off in Las Vegas is a win to players who bet the back line at Lake Tahoe, and if you think you have some money coming and weren't paid off, don't be bashful about having your complaint heard and acted upon right then and there. These matters are always amicably settled to the player's satisfaction, but the player should take the first step.

On the Las Vegas Strip, which is Major League territory in the legal gambling business, most of the Crap-table employees are older men with many years of experience. The big-money players likewise are usually no beginners, and if you're a casual observer without a complete understanding of the game, watching a player make four or five different bets and then get a certain amount of money in one payoff can be quite confusing.

Because neither the players nor the employees elsewhere are expected to make or understand compound mathematical calculations (such as those which take place with speed and accuracy where playing Craps attains its highest refinement), simplified working rules are in effect in some of the casinos. Some require each losing bet to be removed from the table and each winning bet to be paid off in full. Line bets are always paid off that way. Avoiding direct net payments to players reduces the possibility of error by the dealer or the misunderstanding of the payoff by the player. You'll readily see that the peak of proficiency in the handling of bets at a Crap table is not achieved overnight.

I would consider employee efficiency in the gambling

business to be probably no better, no worse, than that in any other business of a financial nature. You'll find all types of employees everywhere. The majority are quietly efficient, a few are outstanding in ability, and a few are definitely below par. I've seen some employed by the biggest and most respected casinos who couldn't do even the simplest mathematical calculations correctly.

In 1960 the journeyman wage for male dealers in the gambling games was $22.50 daily. Qualified female Blackjack dealers began at $90 weekly. These wages would be higher today as a result of recent pay adjustments. The minimum wages are augmented by numerous fringe benefits. Experienced employees earn more from periodic pay raises for length of service, profit-sharing bonuses, and so forth. Beginners or trainees earn less than the journeyman rate during their probationary period.

The question of making extra money through sources other than payments by the employer comes up. This will be bad news to a lot of would-be casino employees who expect to get rich quick, because the evidence shows that there's very little extra money to be had.

"Moonlighting" (concurrently working for two different employers) is not tolerated by the gambling casinos and by the business community at large when employment by a casino is one of those jobs. A drug store clerk, for example, couldn't be a Crap-table dealer on his time off from work at the drug store; a regular casino employee can't hold down a second job as a part-time service station attendant.

Most of the Las Vegas casinos are fully staffed with permanent employees. Experienced dealers can be moved to any part of Nevada on short notice if a casino elsewhere is opening for the summer or expanding its operations. Some of the Lake Tahoe casinos are open during the summer only. It's obviously to their advantage to hire persons who have worked for them before or are known to the management, so employment is on the basis of individual selection by the casino.

Private schools for the training of dice dealers exist. As with similar schools in Florida for the training of baseball umpires, the dice-dealers' schools concentrate on teaching the fundamental rules and practices of the game. They teach what the dealer should do with his left hand and what he should do with his right hand and in what sequence, and what the dealer has to say while he is going through these manual actions. Graduation from a dice-dealers' school is no automatic guarantee of a job, any more than a high school diploma or a college degree is. Dealers have to find jobs after first getting the training for it. In addition, some casinos prefer to train their own dealers.

Those with the necessary know-how and know-whom will step into job opportunities as they exist. All of the casinos like to maintain a roster of available replacements and many of them will give a break to young men and women with no previous experience in gambling, just as the major-league baseball teams will hire a promising youngster just out of school who never played professional baseball.

Shills, employed by some casinos, are used for the purpose of lending an appearance of activity to gambling tables not otherwise patronized. Gamblers are superstitious and consider it bad luck to be gambling alone, and an idle table would remain so until two or more cash customers arrive to begin playing at the same time. Use of a shill attracts the lone player. Some of the shills are bearded and whiskered characters dressed as cowboys or prospectors, and their appearance adds much to the atmosphere of the casinos that employ them.

Stories you may hear that female shills are employed to make big bets to provoke male gamblers into making even bigger ones have no foundation in fact. Shills are usually restricted to bets on which they can win only $1. It is their physical presence, rather than the manner or volume of their betting, that makes them useful to a casino.

I hope these remarks about casino employees, brief as they are, will give you a better appreciation of gambling-casino activity as you may find it when you test your luck at any of the gambling tables. The services of the casino employees at all levels—dealers, supervisory personnel, and top management executives—form the biggest single item in your gambling costs, which are discussed in the next chapter.

CHAPTER 2

EVALUATING YOUR GAMBLING COSTS

Some people think that gambling casinos earn all the money needed to meet their heavy overhead expenses by offering games of chance in which the mathematical advantage very strongly favors the house.

This is true only if you play the high-cost games or make the sucker bets.

It is not even necessary for the house to make anything on any bet to come out ahead and make money. All other things being even, the fellow with the biggest bankroll has the best chance of winning in the long run. Regardless of what the house earns on any game, it is in a preferred position to withstand a run of bad luck simply because it is better capitalized than you, the individual gambler. It will remain solvent in spite of its losses, while any individual suffering a similar stroke of adversity will exhaust his available capital and go broke.

When you go broke you generally tend to remain that way because you have to risk additional cash against the house to try winning any back, and you don't have that extra cash. Besides, a losing gambler is considered one of the world's worst credit risks.

House limits are to protect the casinos. Their only concern about a player's losses is that he be able to pay them. Risking more than you can afford to lose is one of the sins all responsible casino managements warn you against.

If you follow a martingale, or negative-progression system, in your betting, doubling your bet after suffering a loss, that limit on your bets, generous as it is, can soon be reached. It's not a happy feeling to have to quit at a time

when you're far behind in your betting, but if you reach
that stage where you risk the maximum bet to try to recover your losses and come out ahead by one single betting
unit, you've had it! Better to throw in the towel and accept
a technical knockout than to court real disaster with even
one additional heavy loss.

The casino's advantage of being backed by more capital
than any individual gambler is called the "hidden percentage," and it is considered so effective that if all customers
were allowed to gamble free, with no house percentage
favoring the casino, it is estimated that the casinos would
earn nearly as much as they now do. In plain words, gamblers who go broke enable the casinos and the State of
Nevada to remain prosperous.

How to keep from going broke should, therefore, be one
of your primary objectives in gambling, and in Chapter 11
you'll get some advice on how to do this.

The open and intense competition that exists between
legal gambling casinos in Nevada all works to your advantage, giving you an opportunity to compare gambling
costs and payoffs. You will find differences between these
in various casinos, just as you will in the price of food in
grocery stores or gasoline in service stations. Some of those
differences are brought out in this book.

The house percentage on a bet is the percentage that the
casino keeps, on the average, out of the total being wagered by all gamblers making that particular type of bet.
It's a convenient statistical tool for the casino management
because it represents the difference between what it collects
from the gamblers who lose and what it pays off to those
who win, related to the total amount risked. In two-way
bets, where you can bet either for or against a particular
result, each of the positive and negative bets must be considered separately because each has its own house percentage.

While daily income and output figures for a certain
game or type of bet may differ widely and show no

apparent relationship to each other, over any extended period of time they'll average out to show that the house is favored by the calculated house percentage, down to a tolerance of less than $\frac{1}{100}$ of 1 percent.

There are certain labor costs attached to each game and a number of other measurable items (for example, the floor space occupied and the prorated rental or real estate use assessed against the layout, the licenses and taxes for operating that game, and expendable supplies—the dice or cards which frequently have to be replaced). A casino management can, knowing the correct house percentage or, better yet, its rate of earning money, figure with remarkable accuracy how much money must be wagered during a certain period of time for the house to break even on its operating expense for that table. It can also, if it knows how much traffic (in dollars) that table is handling, estimate what its gross income should be, and if it deviates appreciably from the expected profitable result over too long a period of time, it will have good reason to investigate the employees working at that table.

A Roulette layout requiring the services of a croupier and, part of the time, of a pit boss will cost the casino approximately $85 in labor costs during a 24-hour period. A sum of $1614 in cash, or 16,140 chips valued at 10-cents each, has to be wagered each day just to pay the employees who operate and supervise the game. (A second employee, who assists the croupier by counting and stacking chips, is needed only when the Roulette game is heavily patronized.) Add other overhead items, and it is doubtful if one of the big casinos can profitably operate a Roulette wheel for 24 hours with less than $2000 in bets. These labor costs, calculated at the 1960 wage rate, would be higher now.

At a Crap table it must be admitted that this is somewhat complicated due to the many different betting options, but if a Crap table can meet its expenses from the house's advantage figured for the line bets, any other bets giving the house bigger earnings may be considered so much more gravy. Just one player making line bets averaging $10 each, at the rate of 70 per hour, brings an income of about $9.85 to the casino for that hour.

The house, realizing that it might lose several dollars of that income if such a player were to take about fifteen minutes off from his gambling to go to the lunch counter for a cup of coffee or to the bar for a highball, would rather serve those drinks free to the player at the gambling table so the action can go on without interruption than to sell them to the player at the place where they're usually obtained. This accounts for the frequent visits of the cocktail lounge waitresses to the gambling tables. The drinks are offered to all players without discrimination, and if it seems like lavish hospitality on the casino's part, it's also good business.

When hundreds of dollars are changing hands on each roll and the table is crowded with at least a dozen players, many of them making sucker bets which can cost much more than the line bets, the house is clearing its expenses at that table by a wide margin. A big gross income does not necessarily mean a big net income, but it explains why the casinos are able to bid against all outsiders to bring the world's best entertainment to their establishments and give it to the customers either free or at real bargain prices. That same extra money in any illegal gambling setup would be going to bribe the law enforcement agencies and politicians, without whose permission the games could not operate.

The five-figure weekly salaries paid to the entertainment headliners of the day give the impression that, since this money must necessarily come from the customers, gambling is an expensive hobby. This is not so, and millions of people who have never been to Nevada will be pleased to learn that, as I've mentioned before, you can go all-out for maximum enjoyment at the Crap tables for a cost of less than 10 cents an hour. The minute or two you might spend watching the colored lights in a pinball machine can be much better spent in the absorbing game of Craps, in which you not only watch but take an active personal part in what goes on.

In any field of human endeavor in which you're a beginner, the usual procedure is to start small until you acquire some skill in what you're doing. In learning to ski you would, with some understandable injury to your pride, start in on the most gentle slopes where the children are also practicing. You wouldn't take the ski lift to the top of the steepest slope until you had completely mastered the fundamentals of the sport and had the ability to keep the skis under your control at all times.

The biggest mistake made by a beginner in playing Craps is that, instead of controlling his bets, he allows the bets being made by others at the table to control him.

The table minimum also probably plays a part in the gratification of the player's ego. Gamblers who should be playing on tables with a 10-cent or 25-cent minimum are found, instead, on $1 or $5 minimum tables, where their available capital represents a mere shoestring on which to get started. In my original gambling try I made this mistake. I was making $5 bets where even 25-cent bets would have been considered too much for me.

Playing Craps is not expensive to the average player who does it moderately and takes advantage of every possible break he can make for himself. Most of those breaks are in the area of self-discipline, which means, primarily, restricting your betting to the line bets, on which the house earns the least, and betting on the Odds, where the house earns nothing. In the expected frequency of wins and losses if you play both the front line and the back line about equally, out of 288 decisions you should win 140 of them and lose 144. There will be four stand-offs. If you're playing at a 25-cent minimum table and making line bets averaging five 25-cent betting units, those four decisions which can be expected to result in losses in excess of a matching

number of wins and losses will cost you 20 betting units,
or $5. It will take you about four hours to do that much
playing. In addition to your line bets, there will be about
192 rolls where you can bet on the Odds and play what is
literally a game within a game where your chances of
coming out ahead are no worse than an even 50—50 break.
The rest is up to your luck.

Playing Craps, or gambling in any other form in Nevada,
costs you nothing for licenses, club dues, admission charges,
uniforms, special shoes or equipment, locker rentals, or
any of the other expenses commonly associated with recreation. A price of $5 for a gambling session compares favor-
ably with golf, boating, bowling, horseback riding, or any
do-it-yourself activity where, naturally, you expect to pay
someone for providing the equipment or the facilities for
your recreation.

Who said that playing Craps is expensive?

Remember, it's *you* who should decide how much you're
going to bet, within your means, and if you keep your gambling costs down to what you can afford, you'll find that
the "galloping dominoes" offer real enjoyment.

Let's look at gambling costs from another angle.

A contest of luck, the sport of the thing, is of relatively
little concern to the casino and is not needed at all from its
point of view. What management is mainly interested in
is the more certain income it gets as a percentage, commission, fee, service charge, or whatever you want to call
it for providing the mechanical means and facilities for
your gambling and keeping you entertained.

The individual gambler *is* vitally interested in testing his
luck and, to a smaller extent, his skill in playing or managing his betting, or he wouldn't be gambling. The house
accommodates you by covering any bets you want to make
within the limits set by the house for those bets. In doing
so, the house actually risks little or none of its own money.
The money lost by individual gamblers is first collected,
then the winners are paid off out of this, and more often

than not there will be something left over for the house without its having to dip into its own bankroll to make any payoffs.

It's to the casino's advantage for you to play as long as possible, since the casino's real earnings increase with each bet that you make. To offset these earnings by the house you have to come out that much ahead on your luck, a task which all students of gambling and all those who have tried it admit is no snap.

In my extensive studies of the various gambling games I find that the prime factor in any gambler's success is just pure, plain, unadulterated good luck. You don't need much of it to come out ahead if you gamble sensibly, but it has to be there.

I will have to disagree with critics of gambling who describe the house percentage or the cost of gambling to the player as money thrown away. Some people make the same remarks about paying taxes. The really important thing is not so much the cost, which should be kept as low as possible, but what you get for your money. The price you pay for your gambling fun, up to the same amount you would willingly spend on any of your other recreational pursuits, can be considered money well spent for which you received full value.

When that price can be shaved down to less than 10 cents an hour in playing Craps, or nothing at all if you play Faro, gambling as a recreation is certainly within your means.

The amount of capital you can afford to gamble with should be determined by you alone, with respect to your current income or available assets. My suggestion as to the best way to handle this is to write it off in advance as part of your vacation expense. Set the limit which you can lose if your luck goes against you—let's say an amount equal to two or three days' wages—and if you lose that, quit gambling.

When your luck is better than average and you show a

net gain for your efforts, there are various ways to prevent the casinos from winning it all back from you when your good luck begins to run out. I find one of the best is to rush over to a bank or post office and buy a money order to send home. With some of your cash disposed of in this manner, where it won't be lost, you can return to the gambling tables with what's left over and push your luck for still greater gains. In this second stage of your gambling fun you plunge into it with the knowledge that, no matter what the result will be, you'll finish your entire gambling adventure with a net profit.

CHAPTER 3

CRAPS—LINE BETS

You can play Faro and get an even break with the house. Roulette is not subject to any mechanical or functional tampering by the customers. Yet most American gamblers prefer to play Craps in spite of the somewhat shady history of this game.

There must be a reason. What makes Craps so popular?

There are many answers, but among the most important is that by having the opportunity to throw the dice himself, the gambler feels he is taking an active part in shaping his own destiny. This notion will be blasted as pure nonsense by mathematicians and students of gambling, since the skill or brainwork required in throwing the dice is absolutely nil. A three-year-old child or a baby chimpanzee could do it just as well as the most highly educated adult. The only physical strength required is that necessary to throw a pair of dice across the center line of the table with enough force so that they will bounce off the backboard at the far end of the table.

Practice or experience makes no difference either. One who has never played Craps before in his life has just as good a chance of success as a player who spends most of his time at the Crap tables, year in and year out, as far as any particular throw or series of throws is concerned. Nevertheless, the serious gambler goes into the game with a feeling that this will be his lucky day and that he alone is capable of swinging the events of the day in his favor.

Craps provides faster and more satisfying action in a given space of time than any of the other games of chance. It is not rare to see the Crap tables surrounded by a crowd of players and spectators several rows deep while at the same time the Roulette and Blackjack layouts are practically deserted.

Before we get into the action of the game itself, an explanation is necessary regarding the meaning of some of the terms used in describing the game. Some authors refer to a *throw* and a *roll* as being synonymous. Others consider a *roll* and a *hand* as the same things. Consequently, when you read about Craps you're never sure what the author is really referring to when he writes about a roll.

A gaming guide recently distributed by a Las Vegas casino made a noticeable contribution to the understanding of Craps by precisely defining these terms:

A *throw* is one toss of the dice upon the table.

A *roll* is one complete sequence in which the shooter either wins or loses.

A *hand* is the total number of rolls that a player has before passing the dice to the next player.

The word *roll,* restricted to the limited meaning described here, instead of covering anything from a single throw to a shooter's full hand, now begins to make sense.

Decision is often used by gambling authors to mean a roll, probably because of the confusion which surrounds a roll. I prefer to apply the word *decision* exclusively to the last throw in any roll.

I find, in my personal observations at the Crap tables, that few gamblers are familiar with all the rules and practices of the game, and even fewer know the correct odds on each betting option or the price that one must pay to obtain them. This ignorance can be expensive.

The basic bet is a *line* bet that the dice will pass (win), or that they won't. The shooter (the player throwing the dice) is required to make a line bet. He can, of course, make any other bets at the same time.

In betting to pass, or playing the front line, on the first or come-out throw, you win if 7 or 11 (a natural) is thrown; you lose on 2, 3, or 12 (a crap). Any other number—4, 5, 6, 8, 9, or 10—becomes your *point*. To win, your point must be thrown again before a 7 is thrown.

Playing the back line, or betting that the dice won't pass, is exactly opposite from betting on the front line but with one exception. Either the 2 or the 12, as marked on the playing table, is barred, meaning that if the barred number is thrown on the come-out it's a *stand-off* and nobody wins. The barred number enables the casino to maintain its slight mathematical advantage on all line bets no matter which way you make them. If back-line bets were exactly opposite from front-line bets with no barred number it would create an automatic advantage in favor of the player, something which even gamblers themselves admit shouldn't be allowed to happen.

Crap-table covers, by the way, are made to order to the specifications of the casino using them and there is no established rule as to the location of the casino where the barred number is 2 or where it is 12. You'll find both 2 and 12 used in Nevada. Las Vegas uses 12 exclusively, while casinos in other parts of Nevada show a preference for 2 as the barred number.

Let's say that 12 is the barred number; for uniformity we'll stick to that number in all references to back-line betting made in this book. In betting the back line, on the first throw, or come-out, you win on 2 or 3, lose on 7 or 11, and stand-off on 12. Any other number—4, 5, 6, 8, 9, or 10—becomes your point, and to win, a 7 must come up before your point repeats.

Come and *Don't Come* bets are essentially the same as line bets except that they are made anytime during the shooter's roll after the come-out. The next throw after you make your bet is *your* come-out, on which you either win, lose, stand-off, or establish your point for the action to follow. Any bets made before the come-out that the dice will or won't pass are called flat bets. All flat bets pay even money.

Come and Don't Come bets are designed to increase the

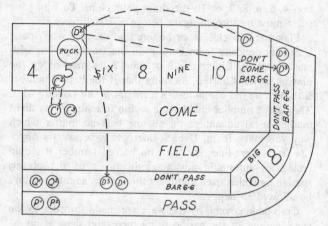

The action on flat bets on the Las Vegas type layout.

total play at the table; the more money in action, the greater the house take. They also serve a psychological need for gamblers whose impatience is such that they can't wait until the next come-out by the shooter, an event that takes place about every third or fourth throw on the average.

Acquaintance with the two types of Crap-table layouts used in Nevada is useful for your better understanding of how the game is played. The Las Vegas casinos use a layout in which there are separate boxes for the Don't Pass and Don't Come bets. The Don't Pass bet made on this type of layout is not moved, and any further action affecting this bet, such as your laying the Odds, or your receipt of your winnings if the dice didn't pass, takes place in the same box.

Pass Bet
 1. Player puts his bet (P¹) in the Pass box.
 2. If the dice pass, player wins. Dealer makes the payoff (P²) alongside.

Don't Pass Bet
1. Player puts his bet (Q^1) in the Don't Pass box.
2. If the dice don't pass, player wins. Dealer makes the payoff (Q^2) alongside. It's a stand-off if the barred number is thrown on the come-out.

Come Bet
1. Player puts his bet (C^1) in the Come box.
2. Dealer moves the bet to the box identifying the point if a point number is thrown on the come-out for this bet. In this example the point is 5. Bet is now located at C^2 in illustration.
3. In the continued action, if the point is thrown again before a 7, player wins. Dealer then returns player's Come bet to where it was originally made (C^1) and makes the payoff (C^3) alongside.

Don't Come Bet
1. Player, if at the extreme end of the Crap table, puts his bet (D^1) in the Don't Come box. If player is anywhere else out of reach of the Don't Come box, he hands his money for this bet to the dealer and the dealer puts it in the Don't Come box for him.
2. Dealer moves the bet to the box behind the point if a point number is thrown on the come-out for this bet. Bet is now located at D^2 in illustration.
3. In the continued action, if a 7 is thrown before the point repeats, player wins. Dealer moves the bet *not* back to the Don't Come box, but to the Don't Pass box nearest the player (D^3). The payoff (D^4) is made alongside.

Pass and Come bets are treated on the Reno layout exactly as they are on the Las Vegas layout. On the Reno layout all the "Don't" bets (Don't Pass and Don't Come) are treated alike.
1. Player puts his bet (D^1) in the box for Don't Pass and Don't Come bets.
2. Dealer moves the bet to the box behind the point if a

point number is thrown on the come-out for this bet. Bet is now located at D² in illustration.

3. In the continued action, if a 7 is thrown before the point repeats, player wins. Dealer then returns player's bet to where it was originally made (D¹) and makes the payoff (D³) alongside.

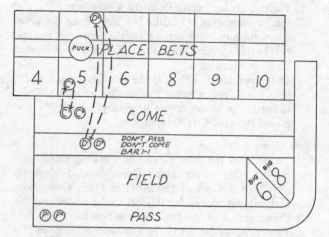

The action on flat bets on the Reno type layout.

On the type of layout preferred in Reno, the Don't Pass and the Don't Come bets are both made in the same box and both are moved back of the point number when a point is established. The box for these "Don't" bets is within easy reach of players. All the flat bets against the dice in Reno are moved out to where the player put his money down, if the player won, and the dealer makes the payoff there.

Before entering any Crap game and making line bets, you're urged to pay special attention to the action going on at the table and particularly to the round marker, or *puck*, which is placed to indicate the point. If a point has already been established and the pending decision is on whether that point or a 7 will appear first, you shouldn't make a line bet just at that time. You can make your bet on Come or Don't Come and the next throw becomes, for you, a come-out and your bet will be treated just the same as if you were throwing the dice yourself and had a line bet on the result.

If you make a bet at this time on the front line, the section marked *Pass,* you're riding for a decision on the point already made by the shooter. You'll only get even money if you win, regardless of what the point is. If a 7 comes up on the first throw after you make what should be a Come bet on the Pass line by mistake, you lose, whereas such a bet properly placed in the Come box would have won. Beginners who are not thoroughly familiar with Craps have been observed to make errors of this type very frequently.

To avoid confusion and to make it easier for them to keep up with the action, most players wait until the shooter is ready to make his come-out. They then make their line bets so the decision on them will coincide in timing with the shooter's own line bet.

You either win or lose on that decision, depending on how you bet and which way the dice went in relation to it.

I've repeatedly seen players lose money on account of having so many bets working at one time that they forget which ones are theirs. In such instances an unattended bet may win several times in succession if no one picks up the money and it's allowed to ride on a similar bet repeated, but as soon as an unfavorable decision is reached the house recovers all the player's winnings plus the amount originally risked. There's always a possibility that some other player, noticing that the player who made the bet is paying no attention to it, will pick up the bet and the winnings or move them to another section of the table where the player who originally made the bet and won it won't recognize it as his money anymore. Until you have had sufficient experience to be able to handle more than one bet at a time, stick to that one bet. Craps is a game where the action is fast—so fast that, for beginners, managing one bet at a time could take up all of their undivided attention.

What are your chances of success on a flat bet?

There are 36 different combinations possible with a pair of six-sided dice. Assuming that the dice are physically perfect, on the average your probability of getting the various scores (sum of the spots on the two dice) out of each 36 throws would be as follows:

Score (Sum of the spots on the two dice)	Frequency out of 36 throws	Possible combinations
2	1	1 + 1
3	2	1 + 2; 2 + 1
4	3	1 + 3; 2 + 2; 3 + 1
5	4	1 + 4; 2 + 3; 3 + 2; 4 + 1
6	5	1 + 5; 2 + 4; 3 + 3; 4 + 2; 5 + 1
7	6	1 + 6; 2 + 5; 3 + 4; 4 + 3; 5 + 2; 6 + 1
8	5	2 + 6; 3 + 5; 4 + 4; 5 + 3; 6 + 2
9	4	3 + 6; 4 + 5; 5 + 4; 6 + 3
10	3	4 + 6; 5 + 5; 6 + 4
11	2	5 + 6; 6 + 5
12	1	6 + 6

In betting to Pass, on the come-out you win on 7 and 11 (total 8 chances out of 36) and lose on 2, 3 and 12 (total 4 chances out of 36). It's 2 to 1 in your favor that you'll win on the come-out as compared to losing on it. On a Pass or Come bet you have an implied contract to let your bet stand until a decision is reached one way or another, and if it isn't decided on the come-out the odds from then on will be against you, since a 7 can come up more frequently than any point you're trying to make.

Conversely, on your betting against the dice, the odds are against the house after the come-out. If your bet is on Don't Pass or Don't Come, you can take it off anytime after the come-out. The casino will be very happy indeed if you do this.

Out of each 36 throws you can figure on an average of three 4s and three 10s. The chances that you'll make your point on either of these are only 1 out of 3. It's 2 to 1 against you after the come-out; a 7 can appear twice as frequently as your point.

You'll have four 5s and four 9s. It's 3 to 2 against you here after the come-out. You'll make your point on an average of 40 percent of the decisions affecting 5 or 9.

There will be five 6s and five 8s. On either of these as a point on a front-line bet, the odds are 6 that you won't make your point against 5 that you will.

All probabilities combined give you the following, out of 36:

	Frequency		Frequency
Come-out:			
Win on 7 or 11	8	Lose on 2, 3, or 12	4
Decision on the point:			
Win on 4 or 10	2	Lose on 4 or 10	4
Win on 5 or 9	3⅓	Lose on 5 or 9	4⅘
Win on 6 or 8	4⁶⁄₁₁	Lose on 6 or 8	5⁵⁄₁₁
	17⁴¹⁄₅₅		18¹⁴⁄₅₅

Reduced to whole numbers which you can more easily understand, your chances of winning or losing a front-line bet or a Come bet are 495 ± 7 (495 plus or minus 7), meaning that you have 488 chances of winning against 502 chances of losing.

The widely advertised house percentage, when expressed as a fraction, is the difference divided by the sum:

$$\frac{251 - 244}{251 + 244} = \frac{7}{495}$$

Decimally this amounts to .014141414141414. For all practical purposes it is not necessary to carry such figures

beyond the third or fourth significant digit. It is drawn out
to fifteen decimal points here merely to compare it fully
with the house percentage on the back-line bets. On that
there is a repeating series of numbers which requires exten-
sion to fifteen decimal points to properly demonstrate it.

Betting on the back line, or that the dice won't pass, is
very slightly more favorable to the gambler. All the probabilities combined out of 35 (not counting the 12, which is
barred) give you the following:

Come-out:	Frequency		Frequency
Win on 2 or 3	3	Lose on 7 or 11	8
Decision on the point:			
Win on 4 or 10	4	Lose on 4 or 10	2
Win on 5 or 9	4⅘	Lose on 5 or 9	3⅕
Win on 6 or 8	5⁵⁄₁₁	Lose on 6 or 8	4⁶⁄₁₁
	17¹⁴⁄₅₅		17⁴¹⁄₅₅

Treated in the same manner as the figures for the front-
line bets just discussed, your chances of winning or losing
on a back-line bet, when expressed as whole numbers, are
1925 ± 27 (1925 plus or minus 27), which means 1898
chances of winning against 1952 chances of losing. The
fraction in favor of the house is reduced to:

$$\frac{976 - 949}{976 + 949} \text{ or } \frac{27}{1925}$$

Decimally the house is favored by .014025974025974.
The house percentage figures are important to you in
one respect. They are related to your probability of winning or losing. If you bet about the same on both the front
line and the back line and figure the house percentage as
the average of 1.414 and 1.403, what you have, 1.408+,
is almost exactly ¹⁄₇₁ of the total amount being wagered.
The house is concerned with the entire action and must
add the expected stand-off on the barred number to say
that its take averages ¹⁄₇₂ of the gross betting total.

As a rough guide you can figure that you'll win 35 and lose 36 out of each 71 line bets that you make (ignoring the stand-offs), and it makes little difference whether you're betting on the front line or the back line exclusively or any mixture of the two. This is one of the best deals a gambler can get in any of the more popular games of chance. The line bets offer such a bargain when compared to other bets that for continuous playing I don't recommend your making any bets that give the house a bigger percentage.

In John Gunther's *Inside Las Vegas* the dice are reported to be thrown once every 16 seconds, on the average, making 225 throws per hour. My own statistical studies show that there are about 3½ throws to each decision and slightly faster activity, which would make the average rate of play about 70 rolls per hour. The rate varies considerably depending on the many factors involved: the number of players, the number of employees serving them, their experience, the type of bets being made, and so forth. When betting is heavy and the dice are running "hot," passing most of the time, there may be a minute or more between throws. At other times, when only two or three players are at a table, the action goes at a fairly fast clip. Thus a casino can earn as much with only three players and speeded-up action as it can with half a dozen of them playing along at the normal rate.

After the come-out, when the shooter throws a 7 instead of his point, he "sevens out," losing the dice, which then go to the player immediately to his left. Any shooter may voluntarily relinquish the dice before he sevens out, and any player can refuse to accept them when it is his turn to be the shooter. The shooter's hand can be terminated by the stick man for infractions of the house rules. The most common of these are applying too little or too much force in throwing the dice. If the dice fail to hit the backboard the shooter will be warned, and if the dice continue to fall short the next player in line of succession to the dice will be asked to take over. Repeatedly throwing the dice so hard that one or both of them fly off the table can also mean loss of the dice to the shooter. The shooter's refusal to make the required line bet at any time automatically terminates his hand.

The final roll in the shooter's hand, in which he sevens out, is also referred to by some authors as crapping out, a rather confusing term in this situation because a crap is 2, 3, or 12, and crapping out, correctly, should refer to throwing a crap on the come-out.

CHAPTER 4

CRAPS—SINGLE-THROW AND HARD-WAY BETS

The field

Besides flat bets there are a number of other betting options in Craps. Some of them are decided on a single throw. On others the action is continuous until a certain result takes place. Some of the bets have a direct relationship to the line bets and the decisions achieved on them. Some are completely independent.

This variety has something to do with the popularity of Craps. The suckers are allowed to choose their own method of being executed, so to speak, and a condemned man given a choice of either being hung or shot by a firing squad is a happier person than one denied that final act of self-determination.

Each type of bet offers you a different probability of success. The payoff roughly corresponds to the risk, but in an amount less than you would get if your entire bet were paid off at correct odds for that risk. The bets with the biggest payoffs appeal most strongly to the suckers. It is no accident that these bets are the most expensive ones.

The bets described in this book are a composite of those observed on all Crap-table layouts I have studied in Nevada. You won't find all of these bets marked on any one table.

Serious gamblers who know the mathematics of the Crap game shy away from almost all of the single-throw bets and leave them to the suckers, who are ever plentiful and always in the biggest hurry to get rid of their money. What's the price of these so-called "sucker" bets? Let's see:

First we'll consider the single-throw bets, or propositions, as they are sometimes called. Single-throw bets can be made *anytime* regardless of the action taking place on the line bets. Because of this fast rate of action and the fact that the probabilities of your losing most of these bets are far above 50 percent, betting heavily on them in relation to your available capital and running into a short streak of bad luck can wipe you out in no more than a minute or two.

On single-throw bets you can bet on probabilities that include 1, 2, 4, 6, or 16 chances out of 36 that you'll win.

Those with 1 chance of success out of 36 can be made on either 2 or 12. All Crap-table layouts are marked with 1–1 and 6–6, usually shown as replicas of the dice.

The advertised rate of payoff is not the same in all casinos, and the same rate may be shown differently on some layouts than on others. If the payoff is 30 to 1, the house percentage is 13⅜. A layout marked 30 *for* 1 is the same as 29 *to* 1, resulting in a 20 percent increase in the house percentage, which is boosted up to 16⅔. A payoff of 31 *for* 1, shown on some layouts, is the same as 30 *to* 1.

A single-throw bet on any of the hard-way scores (with both dice identical), such as 2–2, 3–3, 4–4, or 5–5, can also be made, paying the same as 2 or 12. You have to tell the dealer about it. A *hop* is the term used to designate a single-throw bet, and "hard-way 8 on the hop" is the way you verbally call out a bet on 4–4 on one throw.

Some of the newer Crap-table layouts have the six hard-way possibilities for a single throw marked on them. On these it is only necessary to put your money in the required box for such a bet.

Acceptance of bets on numbers or arrangements not marked on the layout is subject to several conditions. First, the casino must have a policy of allowing it. The dealer has to understand what you're betting on, necessitating some conversation between the bettor and the dealer. Added attention has to be paid to the bet if it is accepted by the house. An employee called the *box man* is assigned to handle it. If the table is crowded with players or if too many of them want to make bets not marked on the layout, the dealer could, either on his own or on orders from his superiors, refuse to accept them. You can see that any dealer's ability to handle bets not listed on the layout, in addition to those that are, is limited.

A Crap table has been described as a perfect place to overcome a feeling of inferiority, because here you can rub elbows with the greats and near-greats in every walk of life under conditions where you're as good as any of them. However, some players will take advantage of the environment at a Crap table to make themselves feel superior. Players who make bets not marked on the layout can be compared to diners who don't want anything on a restaurant menu. What they order has to be prepared exclusively for them at the time. Have you ever noticed anyone bloating his ego in this manner?

On the Las Vegas Strip, where a wealthier type of customer is catered to, mere money brings no distinction. You can bet $100 to $200 at a time in downtown Reno or Las Vegas, where most of the tourists stick close to the table minimum, with some feeling of superiority. On the Strip such bets hardly deserve a second look at the person making them. Even with a small amount of money, if you change from betting on 2 or 12 to calling "hard-way 10 on the hop," you are suddenly transformed in your own estimation from a nobody to a V.I.P. The dealer has to talk to you. The other players notice you also. The higher earnings in tips by employees on the Strip are presumed partly due to customers making these individual and distinctive bets.

The money on these called bets is held by the box man on the unmarked section of the layout immediately in front of him, and if the player wins these bets are paid off before any of the others, giving the impression that the bettor is receiving some special service.

On single-throw bets on 3 or 11, it's 2 chances that you'll win against 34 that you won't, resulting in correct odds of 17 to 1. The casino pays off at the rate marked on the layout, which follows the same pattern used for 2 or 12. The house percentage is $11\frac{1}{9}$ if the payoff is marked 16 for 1 or 15 to 1; it's boosted by half and jumps up to $16\frac{2}{3}$ if the payoff is 15 for 1.

Most casinos will also accept called bets on any odd-numbered score made a selected way or any even number made a selected easy way with the dice not identically spotted, with payoffs the same as on 3 or 11. Acceptance of these bets is subject to the conditions mentioned a few paragraphs back.

The combination of 1 and 2, or 5 and 6, is shown on all Crap-table layouts, and when bets are made on 3 or 11 you can put your money directly on these numbers.

The possible equivalent called combinations are:

                    4 by 1—3 or 3—1
                    5 by 1—4 or 4—1
                    5 by 2—3 or 3—2
                    6 by 1—5 or 5—1
                    6 by 2—4 or 4—2
                    7 by 1—6 or 6—1
                    7 by 2—5 or 5—2
                    7 by 3—4 or 4—3
                    8 by 2—6 or 6—2
                    8 by 3—5 or 5—3
                    9 by 3—6 or 6—3
                    9 by 4—5 or 5—4
                   10 by 4—6 or 6—4

There are three types of single-throw bets involving the probability of 4 chances of winning out of 36, or odds of 8 to 1 against success. They are Any 5, Any 9, and Any Craps (2, 3, or 12). The payoff is 7 to 1, sometimes expressed as 8 for 1, and the house percentage is $11\frac{1}{9}$.

Any 7 carries a $\frac{6}{36}$ probability of winning, or odds of 5 to 1 against it. The payoff is 4 to 1 or 5 for 1 if the layout marks it that way. The house percentage is $16\frac{2}{3}$.

In order to increase the volume of money in action some casinos will pay 16 for 3 if this bet is made in multiples of three betting units. The house percentage is reduced, but by tripling the active money on this bet the house doubles its earnings. Since this possible payoff rate is not marked on any layout, you have to ask about it.

The single-throw bets where you have 16 chances of winning against 20 of losing are Under 7, Over 7, and the Field. The odds are 5 to 4 against you.

Under 7 and Over 7 both pay off even money, and the house percentage on them is $16\frac{2}{3}$.

The Field is the most popular of the single-throw bets and justly so, because it's the only one that falls outside of what you would call sucker bets. In Nevada casinos the Field covers the numbers 2, 3, 4, 9, 10, 11, and 12, on which you win. You lose on 5, 6, 7, and 8. To make this bet more attractive to the players, increased payoffs are made on the 2 and 12.

Authors on gambling whose writings are limited to describing the illegal games outside of Nevada consider that a gambling house is extra generous if it pays off double on both 2 and 12, with even-money payoffs on the other winning numbers. The best elsewhere is not the best in Nevada, and while I make this remark here in regard to bets on the Field, it can be applied to any differences found between legal and illegal gambling. The situation more favorable to the player will always be found in the legal games.

In Nevada the usual payoff on the Field is double on 2 and triple on 12, with even money on other winning numbers. The difference between 20 units taken in and 19 paid out gives the house its expected average earning rate of 1 unit in each 36 throws. The house percentage is $2\frac{7}{9}$.

A payoff of only double on 12 enables the house to keep $2 out of each $36 risked by the players, and its percentage becomes $5\frac{5}{9}$. The casinos on the Las Vegas Strip pay double on 12.

There are several other single-throw bets—marked on a Crap-table layout or made by calling them—that are really a combination of some of those already described.

A dollar thrown on the table with the bettor calling "high-low" is the same as separate 50-cent bets made on both 2 and 12. This bet is placed on the line that separates these two numbers on the layout.

Craps Eleven is a bet split between Any Craps and 11 in equal proportions. On some layouts you'll see the initials C and E, which means Craps and Eleven, but on all tables, whether the C and E are marked or not, you can make this bet. If there's no special place reserved for it, it goes on the line that separates Craps and 11 on the layout.

As a combination bet, Craps Eleven pays 3 to 1 if any crap number (2, 3, or 12) is thrown, and 7 to 1 if 11 is thrown.

The Horn, or the Box, as it is handled in most casinos, is a bet on the numbers 2, 3, 11, and 12 in equal proportions, paying off according to the advertised rate for the winning number.

On 25-cent-minimum tables the minimum amount for the Horn bet is $1. On $1-minimum tables the Horn bet begins at $2. Sometimes you'll see a $5 chip bet with the player calling "Horn bet, high 11." That means there's $1 each on 2, 3, and 12, and $2 on 11.

Be sure to ask the dealer about the Horn bet before you make it. If it's described to you as a bet on which you win $7.50 on a $2 bet, on any of the winning numbers, then you're paying an extra high price for it. This arrangement gives the house a percentage of $20\frac{5}{6}$.

There are limits applicable to single-throw bets which are different from those on line bets. Most casinos with $1-minimum tables will allow you to make proposition bets on anything except the Field and the Horn for 50 cents. The house can pick up your 50 cents as change if necessary, so it will be only using whole dollars in making payoffs. The maximum payoff on any hop can be learned by asking about it. If it's $600, for example, you couldn't bet more than $40 on any number or combination that pays off 15 to 1.

What the house earns as a percentage on the most advantageous of the single-throw bets to the player, the Field (if it pays triple on 12), is twice what it earns on line bets. Since there's action on every throw on the Field and only one decision to every 3½ throws, on the average, on line bets, the house earns only $14\frac{2}{7}$ cents on line bets for every $1 it earns on the Field, for the same amount of money on these bets. For $1 on the table for 252 throws, the house figures to earn $1 if the money is on line bets, and $7 if it's on the Field. Experienced gamblers, knowing this, play the Field only occasionally for minimum amounts.

Hard-way bets are bets that 4, 6, 8, or 10 can be made the hard way, with both dice identical, before the number appears the easy way and before a 7 comes up. It will help you to understand hard-way bets when you know that they are designed to make $1 for the house if you have $1 on these bets over a span of 36 throws. This is the same earning rate that the house enjoys on the Field when 12 pays triple.

The house percentage on hard-way 4 or hard-way 10 is $11\frac{1}{9}$, but because action can be expected in only 9 of the 36 throws, it takes the house as long to earn $1 on this as on the Field, where its percentage is only $2\frac{7}{9}$ but with action on every throw. Hard-way 4 or hard-way 10 pays off 7 to 1.

Hard-way 6 or hard-way 8 has a little lower house percentage, $9\frac{1}{11}$, and correspondingly faster action (11 out of

36 throws), resulting in the same time-period cost to the player as the other hard-way numbers. It pays off 9 to 1.

Because of the higher price for hard-way bets, compared to line bets, careful gamblers usually make them only when they're ahead of the game and when they have a front-line bet on the same point. If your point is 6 and you have $5 on the dice to pass, an additional $1 on hard-way 6 adds some variety and enjoyment to the game.

Many players make bets on all the hard-way numbers at the same time in order to increase their winnings. The risk is also magnified, and a 7 will wipe out all the bets at once. Covering all the hard-way numbers with $1 each over a span of 252 throws will cost you $28. That's a lot of money for a little over an hour's gambling fun. A player starting with only $50, continuously betting $1 each on all of the hard-way numbers, can expect to go broke in less than two hours if his luck is just average, so I advise you to take it easy on hard-way bets.

Crap-table center layouts show the most individuality. Shown here are three of the many distinctive layouts to be seen in Nevada casinos:

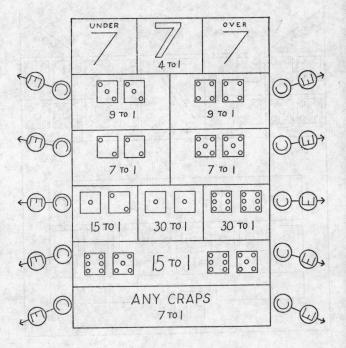

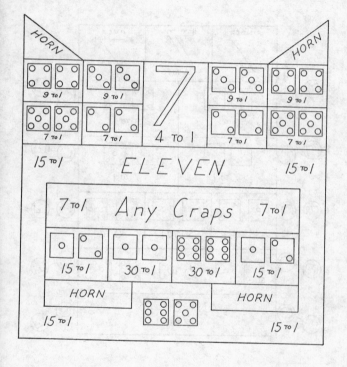

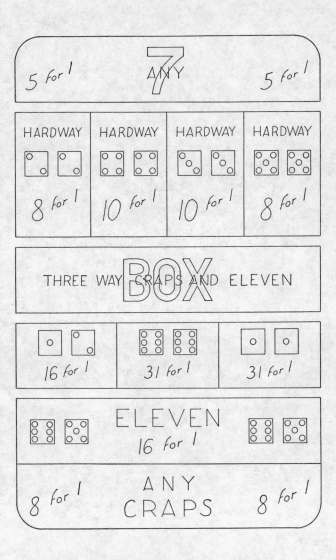

CHAPTER 5

CRAPS—PLACE BETS AND BUY BETS

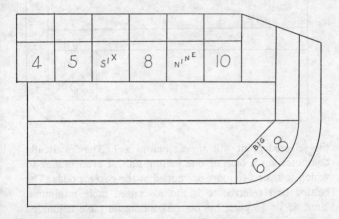

Place bets are bets on a point, but only when you have selected that point yourself (and then placed a bet) instead of making a flat bet and waiting for a point to be established by chance on the come-out throw.

Beginners get confused by place bets. It is important for you to know how they are fiscally computed and how the coins or chips that comprise these bets are actually handled. A knowledge of the two different types of Crap-table layouts used in Nevada brings a better understanding of place bets. The house rules or the individual dealer's preferences may also have to be learned by observation or by asking questions, so that you not only know how these bets are handled but why they are handled the way they are.

Regular place bets are always front-line propositions that

		PLACE	*BETS*		
4	5	6	8	9	10

BIG 6   BIG 8

the selected point will appear before a 7. They're fiscally
computed on a base of one betting unit at even money to
which four or five more are added at the correct odds. The
betting unit referred to is the advertised table minimum.
Your $5 or $6 place bet on a $1-minimum table is handed
to the dealer, since the place bets are put down on a section
of the layout not accessible to players, and the dealer will
put it down on the number you specify.

The bet is usually staggered, with the flat part of the bet
(the unit on which the house pays even money) resting
solidly on the line or in the box reserved for place bets,
and the top money (the additional four or five units on
which the house pays correct odds) offset from the flat
money.

A strict rule for identifying a place bet is to make it
with the top money leaning on an edge of the flat money. It
is made this way to distinguish it from a bet on the Odds,
which is also staggered but in a different manner. The bet
on the Odds will usually be made with the top money level

but with its axis offset about a quarter inch from the axis of the bottom unit.

In actual practice there seems to be little uniformity in adhering to this strict interpretation. Either way is judged correct, and some dealers may be seen handling it one way, others in the other way, in the same casino. The important thing is that the dealer, in handling a place bet in the manner he prefers, know what he is doing. Some concession has to be made for convenience. If there are many bets of the same type in the same box or on the same line, they may all have to be offset in the manner of bets on the Odds, even though the casino would prefer to have the top money leaning on the flat money whenever that is possible. The emphasis on handling place bets at all times is in putting them down on the layout exactly where they belong. This is important because a place bet is often made with a single $5 chip and its location is the only thing that identifies it as a place bet.

The two types of staggered bets are shown here.

On 4 or 10, your betting unit at even money plus four more at correct odds of 2 to 1 results in a payoff of 9 to 5 when you win. On 5 or 9, one betting unit at even money to which four more are added at correct odds of 3 to 2 results in a payoff of 7 to 5. The correct odds on 6 or 8 are 6 to 5, so these have to be added to one unit at even money to make a payoff of 7 to 6. Try to visualize these ratios at all times when you're observing place bets or making them yourself.

Place bets are often misrepresented by dealers who tell you you're getting the correct odds on them. You do, after the first unit at even money, but the full explanation is not made to you.

If your place bet is on the point made by the shooter, as identified by the puck, some casinos will allow you to put it down yourself on the line that marks the beginning of the Pass box on the Crap table. You have to call the dealer's attention to it, and he'll look over your bet to see if the amount and the way the bet is stacked are correct. A single chip couldn't be used in that position. The dealer would either have to substitute five $1 chips for a $5 chip, so the bet could be staggered, or he would have to put the $5 chip in the regular location for place bets.

What is that location?

Now we become concerned with the two different types of Crap-table layouts used in Nevada. These have been designated as the "Las Vegas layout" and the "Reno layout" from the southern Nevada and northern Nevada gambling centers where a certain type of layout is preferred.

On the Las Vegas layout the place bets go on the line that separates the "Do" and the "Don't" boxes for the point numbers on Come and Don't Come bets or on the line in front of the numbered point box. On the Reno layout there is an alley about three inches wide, marked *Place Bets*, instead of a single line. Casino operators in Reno explain that many of the northern Nevada casinos once used the place-bet section of the Las Vegas layout but abandoned it in favor of the one they now prefer when they found that using the Reno layout resulted in fewer errors. The sections for place bets on both types of layout are shown on the following page.

Competent dealers throughout Nevada can handle place bets on either type of layout equally well. The errors result from accidents or mechanical reasons not related to the dealer's first putting place bets down where they belong.

When the bet has to straddle a single line or two very narrowly separated parallel lines on the Las Vegas layout, a single chip can easily be pushed out of position. It can

4	5	SIX	8	NINE	10

PLACE BETS GO
ON
THIS LINE
OR
THIS LINE

		PLACE BETS			
4	5	6	8	9	10

PLACE BETS GO
IN
THIS SPACE

Las Vegas layout (top); Reno layout (lower)

be hit by one of the dice, dislocated by the stick man re-
trieving the dice or by a dealer picking up or moving a
nearby bet.

If a place bet is staggered, the top money offset from the
bottom unit could be toppled for the same reasons, and if
it is not reconstructed in exactly the same manner or in the
same location, the casino will have an argument on its
hands if the player wins and then notices that the character
of his bet has been changed. If the bet is restacked as a
straight pile from top to bottom it will look like a Come
bet, paying even money, and a player who made a place
bet on that point will insist on getting the advertised payoff
for that bet.

It should be explained that Las Vegas dealers, because
of their steadier employment compared to the varying sea-
sonal operations elsewhere, are quite aware of these weak-
nesses on the Las Vegas layout and in spite of a much
greater possibility of accidents the actual occasions for
complaints by players will be very few. In northern Nevada
the relative inexperience of many of the dealers is com-

pensated for to some extent by the wide alley reserved for the place bets.

Your vigilance in seeing that your place bets in any Nevada casino remain unchanged by these unintentional accidents will increase as you gain experience in playing Craps.

When you observe that an accident does happen and your bet has not been properly reconstructed and located by the dealer or stick man, the time to speak up is right away, without delay, to point out how your bet was originally located and stacked. This is not a complaint at this stage but an attempt to avoid a real one, which will surely come if you win your bet and are offered a payoff that does not meet with your satisfaction.

A dislocated $5 chip can result in several possible actions, all unfavorable to you, if not detected and immediately corrected. If the chip gets knocked entirely into the "Don't" section of the box for the point it will be regarded as a Don't Come bet and will be picked up by the dealer as a losing bet when your point is thrown and you should have won on it. If the chip is entirely in the "Do" section of the box for the point, it looks like a Come bet and you'll get even money instead of the advertised payoff for the place bet. You could actually win if your bet accidentally becomes a Don't Come bet from its position in the "Don't" section and a 7 is thrown before your point, but then if you didn't notice the dislocation you're not likely to regard the chip and the payoff on it (made in the Don't Come box) as your money. You would naturally assume that you lost when the 7 was thrown.

The house is always interested in continued action on the table on any bets, and this applies to the place and buy bets as well as any others.

There seems to be one noticeable exception to this policy. It is the practice in many Nevada casinos to take place bets out of action on a shooter's come-out. Very few of the dealers can clearly explain this or the reason for it, except that they are doing it in accordance with the house rules.

It is actually done as a precautionary measure to avoid possible arguments with players. When a shooter "sevens out," all the regular place bets and all the flat bets that the dice will pass, with one exception, are lost at the same time. The last Come (the flat bet on the throw on which the shooter ended his hand) would be a winner for the Come bettor. All the players who made those losing bets know they lost, and there is no misunderstanding about this.

When a shooter throws a 7 on his come-out, however, the result would not be uniform if all bets were working. The dealer would pay off the front-line winners, then he would proceed to collect all the place bets which would be losers. The players who made place bets, hearing the dealer cry out "seven—a winner!" may assume that they too should be winners, or at least not losers, because they are also betting on the dice to pass as far as the points for their place bets are concerned. Many players like to keep their place bets working as long as the same shooter holds the dice, up to his final throw when he sevens out, and will request that their place bets be off on come-outs. The house, in taking the initiative on this, does for many players what it believes the players would want themselves. The house has its own reasons. You can call it insurance if you like. The house is willing to lose part of the action part of the time to avoid losing all of it for an indefinite period.

The place bets are not the only bets on the table, and by having them off on a come-out the house loses action on this segment of the betting for about sixteen seconds. If there is an argument by a player who can't understand why he lost a bet, it ties up the action at the table. Playing at other tables stops too as the players all crowd around to see what the dispute is about. It takes a lot longer than sixteen seconds to settle an argument.

The house will earn the gratitude of players who didn't know this house rule which could be working in the players' favor. On the other hand, there is a possibility of an argument by a player who perhaps had a place bet up on 10, when a shooter after making some other point then comes out for a new roll and throws a 10.

I make this statement, which I repeat many times throughout this book, that an intelligent player in any casino game should become acquainted with the house rules that affect all of his betting, and at the same time should advise the dealer of his own intentions if he makes decisions that are exceptions to the usual way his bets are handled. The house usually wants your place bets on, but you can have them off anytime you request it. Conversely, if the house wants to take place bets off on come-outs, you can have yours working if you ask to have them handled that way.

When you win a regular place bet you will be offered your winnings in the Come box on the layout. The original bet remains where it is and won't be removed unless you ask for its return. If you don't want to continue making that same place bet, tell the dealer that you want to "drag it down." He will then take it off the line or out of the place-bet alley and hand it to you. Since your intention is to take it off the table entirely, it's usually given to you in a hand-to-hand transfer rather than by moving it out to the Come box. Your winnings on place bets will be handed directly to you if you request it.

A situation often confusing to observers is in watching a player get handed less than the amount he won. This is easily explained. The player wants to "press" his place bet, which means increasing it after a win. Therefore, when a player wins $7 on a $5 place bet on 5 or 9 and wants to "press" it, the dealer will put a $5 chip on top of the one already working and hand the player the $2 difference. The player now has a $10 place bet on which he may win $14.

On tables with a $1 minimum, place bets are usually accepted for $3 on any of the points, paying off $5 on 4 or 10, $4 on 5 or 9, and $3.50 on 6 or 8—that is, if half-dollars are handled in payoffs. Otherwise, the wager on 6 or 8 will have to be made for the full $6. You don't get all the advantage of the correct odds on these $3 place bets on 4, 5, 9, or 10, because after the first $1 at even money there are only two more dollars on which you can get the correct odds, compared to four more when you're betting $5. The bet on 6 or 8 for $3, if it's permitted, is simply half of the regular $6 bet. The difference between $3 and $5 is so small that any player who makes place bets should go in for them for the full amount.

Also on $1-minimum tables you may see a player spreading out a single dollar on each of the points. That dollar on each point is the flat money dollar with no additional money at correct odds. This particular spread is usually "off" on all come-outs by the shooter and "on" on all throws after the come-out. These are relatively unwise bets to make. Any player who will accept even money on a pure 2 to 1 risk against him on 4 or 10, for example, exhibits a fundamental weakness in reasoning.

Big 6 or Big 8 is classified here for what it actually is—a place bet. It pays off even money. It is considered a sucker bet of the first magnitude not for its cost, which is a moderate one, but for the fact that essentially the same bet can be made as a regular place bet at one sixth of that cost.

Some critics of gambling complain that dealers should advise players not to bet on Big 6 or Big 8 and to make place bets on those numbers instead. The need for the suckers to be educated is universally admitted, but it's not the dealer's job or duty to tell players how they should or should not bet. The dealer is paid to conduct the game according to the house rules and to handle customers' bets any way the customers want to make them.

I've often asked players who bet on Big 6 or Big 8 why they do it. The reason most often given to justify this bet is that it can be taken off anytime. If the players knew more about Craps they would know that all the place bets are revocable.

Commission, or *buy,* bets, appropriately named because you pay an added percentage for the privilege of getting the correct odds on your bet, are place bets that can be made either way—on or against any selected point. A commission of 5 percent is charged against the short end of the bet and is payable at the time you make the bet. To give you full value for the commission, the short end of your bet should be for not less than twenty times the amount of the commission.

If you're betting large amounts the minimum commission presents no special problem, but for the average gambler whose maximum bet seldom equals or exceeds $10 there will be differences observed in the minimum commission charged or the minimum buy bet allowed. Some casinos have a rigidly imposed minimum commission of $1, which applies to all tables even though some of them have lower limits on line bets. Others calculate the minimum commission as being the same as the table minimum, so if you're playing at a 25-cent-minimum table you can buy 4 or 10 for as little as 25 cents for a $5 bet. Buy bets to pass on 5, 6, 8, or 9 are not recommended. The regular place bets on these numbers cost you less.

You might be allowed to split the minimum buy bet among the two numbers carrying an equal risk. Instead of $20 on a single number, let's say 4, you could buy bets of $10 each on 4 and 10. Any concession made by a casino in lowering the minimum bet ordinarily allowed on any number is for the purpose of encouraging play at the table. If it's a question of getting action on your $20 as $10 each on 4 and 10, or not getting it at all, the casino will lean over backwards in its desire to please you and, not so incidentally, earn a dollar for itself.

Don't hesitate to ask the dealer to explain the minimum commission or the minimum amount of buy bet you can make, every time you play, since this can vary at different times in the same casino.

If your buy bet is on 4 or 10 you hand the amount of your bet plus the 5 percent commission to the dealer, telling him what the money is for. He'll put down your bet either in the position for a regular place bet or in the same box on the layout where Come bets go after the come-out on them. A small round or rectangular chip imprinted "Buy" put on top of your bet identifies it as a buy bet on which the commission has already been paid. Some casinos use a half-dollar to mark the buy bets.

If your bet is against any point number you hand the dealer the commission and 1⅕, 1½, or 2 times what you hope to win, depending on the point you're betting against, and the dealer puts your bet behind the number in the same box where Don't Come bets go after the come-out on them. You can make these bets in any amounts larger than the minimum as long as the expected payoff and the commission are in amounts that the house can conveniently handle. If no coins smaller than whole dollars are handled at a table on payoffs, make sure you're trying to win a sum that comes to an even-dollar amount with no cents left over.

Your winnings on a buy bet on 4 or 10 are put in the Come box. Your winnings on a buy bet against any of the point numbers are put in the Don't Come box. If you want to drag down the bet, that too will be moved out to where your winnings are. Or, if you prefer, the dealer will hand your bet and your winnings directly to you.

In your winning a buy bet which is being repeated, the house will have to collect another commission for the bet that remains active because the house earned the commission on your previous bet from the decision on it. Therefore, when you win $20 on a buy bet against any of the point numbers and you don't drag down your bet, you'll actually receive $19 as the $20 payoff less the commission. The dealer should make it clear to you that he's retaining $1 for the commission on the currently active bet.

Buy bets, like the other place bets, are removable any-time before a decision is reached on them. If you decide to drag down your bet, both the amount of the bet and the prepaid commission will be returned to you. The house earns that 5 percent commission only when there is winning or losing action on your bet.

Sometimes big-money bettors spread out place bets on all the point numbers (or on those not the shooter's point if the bettor also has a front-line bet working on it at the same time) in an attempt to increase their winnings. The multiple risk is consolidated in a gamble against the num-ber 7 coming up, and a shooter who sevens out causes all those bets on point numbers to be lost at one time.

The puck which marks the point made by the shooter is reversible. The top is either blank or shows the word "On." The bottom has the word "Off." When players have a big spread of place bets, they don't want to lose them all if the shooter throws a 7 on his come-out. Taking off or removing all the place or buy bets from the table every time the shooter comes out, and replacing them in time for the next throw if a decision is not made on the come-out, is a physi-cal task that would drive both dealers and players crazy. Reversing the puck makes this maneuver possible without having to do it the hard way. The puck with the word "Off" has the effect of temporarily dragging down all your place or buy bets; reversing it again to show "On" means that those bets are once again working.

One improvement is the use of a puck which is a large ring instead of a flat disc. Small, brightly colored tokens about the size of a half-dollar, with the words "Bet Off" on them, can be put on any bets temporarily removed from action. Thus, if some gamblers want their place bets off and others don't, all can be satisfied by this selective ac-tion. It also applies to any selected single bets out of a greater number of them made by the same player.

In this way a gambler who makes a spread of place or buy bets on all the points, either independently or in addition to the point covered on a front-line bet, can have his bets working as long as the same shooter holds the dice. Rolls of at least 20 throws before a decision is reached are not unusual, and on those occasions when a shooter is really "hot" and holds the dice for an hour, 150 throws, more or less, can be counted on after come-outs, of which about 100 will be winners for the gambler who has all the point numbers covered. You can readily see that a big-money bettor covering each point with the maximum bet allowed by the casino can clean up anywhere from $50,000 to $100,000 in an hour's fast and furious action.

Full, regular place bets on all the point numbers can be made for 32 betting units for the spread. If they're "Off" on come-outs, the complete spread can be expected to earn 60 betting units for the house over a span of 252 throws, requiring a little over an hour's time on the average. These spreads clearly should not be attempted if they tie up all of your available capital, because your luck must be immediate and it must be substantial if you hope to finish a big winner.

On a 10-cent-minimum table you can try it on a more modest scale for only $3.20. Your gains or losses will be proportional to the 50- or 60-cent place bet on each point, but the personal excitement will be as great as ever regardless of the amount you risk.

The gamble on any of these spreads covering all the point numbers is that at least four or five points will be made before the shooter sevens out. Sometimes you may not be making the spread for the purpose of stretching your luck until it runs out and you'll want to quit after only a few wins while you're still ahead. Just tell the dealer you want all your place bets "Off," he'll reverse the puck or put a "Bet Off" marker on each bet, and then if you ask for the return of your money it will be handed back to you with no risk that you'll lose any of it if the shooter sevens out while some of your money still remains on the table.

Mention of what the house earns on place bets has been deferred up to now. It was felt that you can better grasp the mechanics of place betting without getting too deeply involved in mathematics while learning something new.

On place bets the house percentages, as such, are a correct evaluation of the casino's earnings or the cost of playing to the gambler only in a very limited sense. The question of how often there is action on the type of bet made also enters into the picture.

From the casino's point of view, if a player has $1 at even money on the table through 36 throws, the expected earnings are $1 if the bet is on 6 or 8, $2 if on 5 or 9, and $3 if on 4 or 10. When you add the extra $4 or $5 on which you get correct odds, the average price per dollar risked on a full regular place bet is a small one. The casino counts on a volume of business to boost its income.

The house could earn money in the same amount as it does on $5 place bets on 4, 5, 9, or 10, or $6 place bets on 6 or 8, if it accepted place bets of $5 *against* 6 or 8 (paying $4); $8 *against* 5 or 9 (paying $5); or $11 *against* 4 or 10 (paying $5).

I've asked questions in numerous casinos and have yet to find one that will accept these "negative" place bets. Gambling professionals like to use the term *without guts* to describe players who are afraid to take risks. Here it is the casino managements who are the ones without guts. What are they afraid of? One would think that with the house earning the same amount of money whether a full place bet is for or against the point, it would give you the opportunity to bet either way, and wouldn't care how you bet as long as it got the action.

On buy bets, the commission itself is the casino's gross profit margin.

Place bets serve a useful purpose as a hedge against any errors you may have made in your betting. Players following a "system" sometimes lose track of how much or where they should make their next bets. You can't remove any money put down on the table on a front-line (Pass or Come) bet, but if you find you bet the wrong way or in an incorrect amount, greater than you intended, after the come-out a buy bet may be made against the point in the amount needed to offset that error. If your wrong bet was on the back line, you can drag it down after the come-out and then either place or buy the point if that too is necessary.

In making place bets or buy bets, always be sure to bet first on the Odds on your point on any flat bet you may have working, up to the maximum amount that the casino will allow you to bet on the Odds. Why pay for something you can get free?

Here's how the place and buy bets compare:

Bet	HOUSE'S ADVANTAGE ON PLACE BETS		HOUSE'S ADVANTAGE ON BUY BETS	
	Fraction	Percent	Fraction	Percent
On 6 or 8	$\frac{1}{66}$	$1\frac{17}{33}$	$\frac{1}{21}$	$4\frac{16}{21}$
On 5 or 9	$\frac{1}{25}$	4	$\frac{1}{21}$	$4\frac{16}{21}$
On 4 or 10	$\frac{1}{15}$	$6\frac{2}{3}$	$\frac{1}{21}$	$4\frac{16}{21}$
Against 6 or 8			$\frac{1}{25}$	4
Against 5 or 9			$\frac{1}{31}$	$3\frac{7}{31}$
Against 4 or 10			$\frac{1}{41}$	$2\frac{18}{41}$
Big 6 or Big 8	$\frac{1}{11}$	$9\frac{1}{11}$		

CHAPTER 6

CRAPS—BETTING ON THE ODDS

In the preceding chapters you have seen how some of the betting options in Craps differ from one another and how the most expensive of those discussed so far cost the gambler nearly fifteen times the least expensive in terms of the house percentage that the casino enjoys on his bets, and over fifty times in terms of the amount that the house earns in any measured period of time.

Where you can save money right from the beginning is in avoiding the sucker bets entirely, playing the borderline ones with caution if at all and only for minimum amounts, and concentrating your attention on the line bets, which are the most advantageous ones for you to make.

A gambling casino has to charge for its services in providing the facilities for your gambling and can't be playing Santa Claus to all who would like to gamble absolutely free. It will come as most pleasant news to you to learn that, as a bonus to you for making line bets, the ones on which there is the least house percentage, Nevada casinos will allow you to wager *more* money with no cost whatever to you for obtaining the correct odds on it.

A betting option very little known by amateur gamblers and rarely mentioned in any of the free literature distributed by the casinos is the practice of *betting on the Odds*.

This is a supplementary bet related to the flat bets. When a decision is not made on the come-out and the action continues for or against the established point, a player having a flat bet is allowed to make a bet on the Odds on his point in exact ratio to the probability that the point will or won't be made.

While line bets are usually mentioned in reference to betting on the Odds, Come or Don't Come bets are equally affected by any comments in this book concerning line bets.

Before we proceed any further, some definitions are in order. The word *odds* in gambling literature is confusing unless the author carefully defines what he means by it. In the ordinary sense it is the probability of failure in a given risk compared to the probability of success. The first figure given in an odds ratio is always the one for the probability of failure. A success probability of 1 chance in 10 is the same as odds of 9 to 1.

In each of the three different point groups in which betting on the Odds can be done—4 or 10, 5 or 9, 6 or 8—those odds (that a 7 will be thrown before the point) are respectively 2 to 1, 3 to 2, and 6 to 5.

The answer to the question "What odds are you giving?" is different because that one refers to the amount of money or the ratio between the amount you risk and the amount the party you're betting against risks, and it may have only a remote resemblance to the true probability of failure or success. On baseball parlay tickets, which are sold legally in Nevada and illegally everywhere else, under "Parlay Odds" is the notation that nine teams pays 60 to 1. Your probability of picking the names of nine baseball teams at random and having them win all their respective games against other teams not in your selection on that day is one chance in 512, or odds of 511 to 1.

Fortunately, in betting on the Odds in Craps you get the correct payoff for the risk you're taking. The odds on the risk, both statistically as a probability and materially as the amount you can win, are identical.

In any bet other than at even money, the bettor risking the lesser amount is holding the *short end* of the bet. Any bet in which the bettor risks more than he can win is an *odds-on* bet. You sometimes hear of this term in horse rac-

ing when the favorite is so heavily backed in the betting
that the payoff for a $2 pari-mutuel ticket is less than $4.
In other words, you risked $2 to win $1.90 or less.

Craps is unique among popular American gambling-
casino games in allowing players to make bets (buy bets
against a point, or bet on the Odds against a point) that
offer the gambler a better than 50 percent chance of
winning.

Gamblers generally shy away from odds-on bets, perhaps
from superstition, and it is difficult to induce gamblers to
make them even when the payoff is the correct amount for
the risk they're taking. It always seems more agreeable to
win $6 on a $4 risk than to win $4 on a $6 risk.

The bettor holding the short end of the bet *takes* the
Odds, and the bettor holding the long end or making the
odds-on bet *lays* the Odds.

As already stated, you make your bets on the Odds as a
supplement to your line bets. If you're betting on the front
line your bet on the Odds must also be that the dice will
pass, or, more properly speaking, since a point has already
been established, that the shooter will make his point. You
put your bet on the Odds on the unmarked portion of the
Crap-table layout in front of you, directly behind your line
bet but on your side of the line that marks the beginning of
the Pass box. Your bet on the Odds when made here can
be in a straight pile. No other type of bet goes on the table
at this location.

On a Come bet, when a point is thrown on the come-out
for it, that bet will be moved by the dealer to the box that
marks your point on the layout. You have to hand the
money for your bet on the Odds to the dealer serving your
part of the table, telling him what the money is for. Usually the words "on the Odds" are sufficient. This calls for
some quick thinking and manual dexterity because the action at a Crap table is so fast that the slightest hesitation will
cause you to be too late for the next throw.

The bet on the Odds as an adjunct to the Come bet is

staggered. In actual practice there is no strict adherence to any rule that all bets on the Odds must be identified in a specified manner, and like the place bets discussed in the previous chapter, a bet on the Odds will be identified by the dealer in the manner either he or his employers consider most convenient for speed and accuracy in handling it.

We'll illustrate with an example of the $3 Come bet. The point is 6. The player wants to take the Odds for $5, to try to win $6 more if his point is thrown before a 7.

He hands his $5, either as five $1 chips or a single $5 chip, to the dealer and tells the dealer to put it on the Odds.

The dealer can stack the $5 on top of the $3, offsetting it slightly to identify the top money as the bet on the Odds.

The same bet on the Odds can also be handled in a separate stack if it consists of more than one unit, with the top money leaning on an edge of the bottom unit or level on top of it but offset. Either way is correct as long as the dealer is able to distinguish the bet on the Odds from the

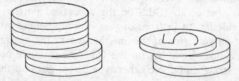

Left—A $3 Come bet topped by five $1 chips on the Odds.
Right—A $3 Come bet topped by a $5 chip on the Odds.

Come bet it is next to, and of course also from any place bets on that point. House rules in some casinos require inexperienced dealers to keep the bets on the Odds separate from the flat bets at all times.

There are some advantages and disadvantages to any method chosen. If both the flat bet and the bet on the Odds are stacked in the same pile with the offset marking the

Either of these staggered stacks, put next to a flat bet and in the same box with it, is a bet on the Odds. The entire bet, including the bottom unit, is paid off at the correct odds for the risk.

division between the two, you would have a rather unstable stack of coins or chips that could be easily toppled over. If the bet on the Odds is handled as a separate staggered stack close to the flat bet, more than twice as much room on the layout is required. The dealer, if experienced and allowed to use his own discretion, could handle it one way at one time and another way at another time, depending on the conditions prevailing on each occasion.

If you take or lay the Odds on Come bets, an exchange of information between you and the dealer is advisable. First, you should inquire whether it is the house's policy to take the Odds off automatically or leave them working on a shooter's come-out. Then, if you want to follow a policy that is different, you should advise the dealer what your intentions are. It is your privilege to take the Odds off or have them working at any time, but the dealer won't know how you want this handled unless you tell him.

When a player lays the Odds in connection with a Don't Pass or Don't Come bet, there is more than one correct way of handling the bet on the Odds. The dealer will do what he thinks is best under the circumstances. If the short end of the bet on the Odds (the amount the player expects to win on it) is the same as the flat bet, the dealer could make a pile equal to the flat bet next to it, and the excess could straddle the two piles. The dealer, in making a payoff, ignores the excess and merely matches the two stacks that arise from the table surface.

If many coins or chips are involved, the bet on the Odds

$4 Don't Pass or Don't Come bet (the point is 5 or 9), with the player laying $6 on the Odds at single odds. The dealer matches the two $4 stacks when making a payoff.

by itself could be handled in this manner if the expected payoff for it comes to an even number of units. The expected payoff on the Odds will be split into two equal stacks and the excess will straddle them.

As you acquire some experience in making bets on the Odds, when you make a flat bet you'll have the amount for any probable bet on the Odds already in your hand ready to put down on the table in front of you or hand to the dealer as soon as a point is thrown.

This is no time to be fumbling around in your pockets for money or asking the dealer to give you coins or chips

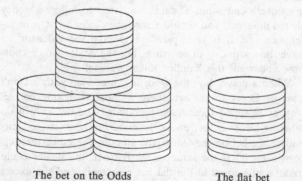

The bet on the Odds   The flat bet

$10 Don't Pass or Don't Come bet (the point is 5 or 9), with the player laying $30 on the Odds at double odds. The dealer matches the three $10 stacks arising from the table surface when making a payoff.

in exchange for your currency. Let's say that the point is 6, you have $2 on the front line, and you want to take the Odds for your $2.50 against the $3 you might win from the house on it. You don't have the two and a half dollars required, but you do have a $10 bill. Put that $10 bill down on the table in the location for your bet on the Odds, or hand it to the dealer if you're taking the Odds on a Come bet, calling out "two-fifty on the Odds!" as you do it. If you don't know the exact amount necessary, call out "full Odds!" The dealer will recognize your bet and it will be effective even if the shooter throws your point on the next throw while the dealer still has your $10 bill in his hands. The vitally important thing is that you showed your money and weren't afraid to risk some of it.

All Crap-table layouts have the words "no call bets accepted" on them. This refers, not so much to verbally announcing your bets or your intention of making them, which is sometimes necessary, but to calling out bets without producing the cash and letting go of it to signify that you're taking a risk.

If you put more down on the table or hand more to the dealer than an announced bet actually requires, you'll be paid off the proper amount for your win on the announced bet, and the $10 bill, if we refer to the above example, will still be yours. If you lost $2.50 because the shooter sevened out before throwing your point, the dealer will give you $7.50 change.

The action in your making flat bets and betting on the Odds follows essentially the same sequence as that illustrated for the line bets, except that when you add your bet on the Odds after the come-out you have two separate bets that will be affected by the same decision. When you're paid off for your win there will be at least four different groups of coins or chips for you to pick up. My observation is that many players fail to recognize all of it as their money or are so slow in picking it off the table that some of it gets caught there when the shooter throws the dice again. This, of course, favors the house, which is interested in getting as much continued action with your money as possible, and is the reason why flat bets and bets on the Odds, and all bets generally, are paid off in the Pass, Come, and Don't Pass boxes.

On the Reno layout, if you're betting against the shooter making his or your point, you hand your money for your bet on the Odds (you're laying them) and the dealer will put it in the box next to your Don't Pass or Don't Come bet back of the point number. On the Las Vegas layout you might be allowed to put your bet on the Odds down next to your Don't Pass bet yourself. Bets on the Odds on Come bets on both types of layout have to be handed to the dealer.

You have to be patient in betting on the Odds if the dealer has to handle your bet because, first, the dealer must pick up the bets that lost and pay off the winners before he can accept any new bets. Then too, he is occupied with such related duties as making change, dragging down bets that players want temporarily or permanently removed from action, and so forth. On a busy table with many gamblers making a wide variety of bets, some action of a paying or receiving nature takes place on every throw of the dice —a lot of it, of course, after those throws which result in a decision that the shooter won or lost on his line bet. As soon as this action has been completed, don't be timid about attracting the attention of the dealer, who is expected to serve you. There may be other players competing for his attention also. The dealer is not a mind reader and he'll welcome your telling him what the money is for when you hand it to him.

If you bet on the Odds on every possible occasion for the maximum that the casino will allow you to bet (in relation to the amount of your flat bet), the dealer will expect your bet when it is due and the exchange of cash or chips between you and him can take place without the necessity of any further conversation about it when you hand him the exact amount for your bet.

When your bet on the Odds is that the shooter will throw your point before a 7, your taking the Odds means that what you bet on them will win you 2, 1½, or 1⅕ times your bet depending on what the point is.

Betting on the Odds is restricted to players having flat bets. Very rarely an exception may be made in the case of one player staking another (furnishing the money for his gambling) or perhaps a husband and wife, playing at the same table, who may be considered as one for betting purposes. Under the circumstances, for example, the husband could make a bet on the Odds in connection with his wife's line bet if she neglected to do so herself. If there are relatively few players at a table and the dealer gives his consent to this, it is all right. However, don't attempt it or even ask to do it at a very busy table, because the dealers have enough to do and think about already without getting involved in trying to remember who is betting for someone else.

Some casinos in Reno and on the north shore of Lake Tahoe allow you to play for *double odds,* and if you have the opportunity to do so, by all means take advantage of it because this concession by the casino does not add anything to your gambling costs. If luck is with you, it will enable you to win much more than you would with only single odds.

You can sometimes *press,* or increase, your bets on the Odds beyond the amounts ordinarily allowed. This is done for the convenience of the casino so that your bet or the casino's payoff, or both, will be in whole betting units or dollars with no fractional parts left over.

When the point is 6 or 8, a line bet of five betting units would allow you to take or lay 5 against 6 on the Odds. If you have four or sometimes only three betting units on the line, with single odds, or two on the line with double odds, you'll be allowed to make the 5 against 6 bet on the Odds.

All of the Las Vegas casinos allow it with three betting units on the line.

Thus, on a 10-cent-minimum Crap table, by making the minimum bet of only a dime, if you're playing for double odds you can make bets on the Odds on any point that may come up, even if it is 6 or 8. The house will allow you to take 25 cents against 30 cents or to lay 30 cents against 25 cents. This is more than double odds.

Whether a casino will allow you to do this for bets higher than the table minimum comes under the jurisdiction of the house rules. You would assume that if you can take 25 cents against 30 cents on the Odds in connection with a 10-cent line bet, when the point is 6 or 8, you could do the same thing, multiplied a hundred times, when you're playing with $5 chips. With a $10 line bet, full double odds would be $20 against $24, and some casinos will limit your double odds to exactly twice what you have on the line. Other casinos will stretch their limits and let you press your bet on the Odds to $25 against $30. Whatever the limit on this interpretation of double odds, always make your bet for the maximum ratio that the casino will allow.

If the point is 5 or 9 and you have an uneven number of betting units on the line, most casinos will let you boost the short end of your bet on the Odds to the next even number, for single odds. Three dollars on the line will allow you to take or lay $4 against $6. The house would rather have you bet this way than bet $3 against $4.50, where the half-dollar introduces the possibility of an error in handling the money. The same bet at double odds or a doubled bet ($6 at single odds) might only entitle you to take or lay $6 against $9. Then again, if the casino allows the initial step-up as an across-the-board ratio applicable to all bets not exceeding the table maximum, $4 against $6 could be doubled to $8 against $12. It all depends on the house rules prevailing at the time.

With 4 or 10 as the point, no further adjustment is needed in the ratio for a bet on the Odds. Your taking or laying 1 against 2 automatically takes care of almost all situations. On a $1-minimum table where only whole dollars are paid out on payoffs, your bet on the Odds against 4 or 10 would have to be in an even number of dollars to result in whole-dollar payoffs.

Sometimes on $1-minimum tables where single odds are allowed, when you have $1 on the front line and the point is 5 or 9, the dealer will explain that you can take the Odds for $2 against $3 if you also add $1 to your line bet. This is a sucker trap. The extra dollar you add to your line bet only wins you even money, a relatively high price to pay for the privilege of getting the correct odds on the $2 behind the line. Besides, if the table pays out half-dollars you could take the Odds for $1 against $1.50 without adding anything to your gambling cost. Therefore, your extra dollar on the line only gets you correct odds on another dollar back of the line. If you want to put some extra money on 5 or 9, beyond the maximum that you can put on the Odds, make the regular place bet for the full amount of $5.

All casinos impose minimum and maximum limits on the line bets a player can make. There are also limits for betting on the Odds, and they may be different from those for the line bets. The short end of the bet on the Odds would be the figure to which the limit applies. If you don't see a notice on the Crap table itself or hanging above it or on the wall nearest to it, it doesn't hurt to ask what the limits are on the table where you're playing. You may never bet that much, but it's always a good idea to know what that limit is, just as the driver of a motor vehicle should be acquainted with the speed limits on the highways. In some of the downtown Las Vegas casinos, on tables with 10-cent- or 25-cent-minimum line bets, you can't bet on the Odds with less than $1 on the line.

On tables with $1-minimum line bets it is often not possible to make bets on the Odds for small amounts and have the expected payoffs come to exact whole-dollar figures. A table with a 50-cent, 25-cent or 10-cent minimum (the lower the better) is preferable even when you usually bet much more heavily than the table minimum, because it enables you to take advantage of betting on the Odds on every possible occasion for the greatest amount in each instance.

Since about one third of the decisions in Craps are made on the come-out, betting on the Odds is possible in the remaining two thirds of the rolls.

One would assume that what you win or lose by betting on the Odds would be about two thirds of the amount of your gains or losses on the line when you play for single odds. In my extensive studies covering the equivalent of an individual's full-time gambling at the Crap tables for over six years, very early in my research I found that what I was winning on the Odds exceeded my gains on the line by 20 percent. These figures are based on playing for single odds, figured from the short end of the bet, and would be greater when the betting on the Odds is for more than the amount of the line bets.

Repeated studies made since this significant original observation confirm that, with average luck, for each $100 you're ahead on the line you'll win another $120 on single odds even though you have your bets on the Odds made in only about two thirds of the rolls. When you lose on the line you can expect some losses on the Odds too; here again the situation on betting on the Odds was found more favorable to the player than the line bets. The losses on the Odds usually amounted to less than the losses on the line.

There has to be a balance somewhere, and it took a great deal of study to find where it is. You have to run into very, very bad luck to observe what happens in such cases. If insufficiently capitalized, you probably won't hold out against a continuous streak of your worst luck long enough to learn much about it in actual gambling in Nevada, but in a statistical project your bad luck costs you nothing and leads to some information valuable to you.

If your luck is simply terrible, which could happen to any of us anytime, you'll have *increased* losses on the Odds which will offset the moderate gains made when your luck is about average. When your line bet is on Don't Pass or Don't Come and you're playing for double odds and laying three or four times your line bet to try to win something extra, it really hurts to have the shooter make your point when your bets are that he won't. A single loss in itself may not be disastrous, but when the same thing repeats a number of times it will cost you plenty, either in real cash in Nevada or in statistics marked down on a piece of paper.

You can count on losing this type of bet in about one third of your bets against the dice involving 4 or 10 as the point. Your chance of losing three such bets in succession without any wins to compensate for the losses is 1 out of 3 cubed or $\frac{1}{27}$, a fairly remote possibility but nevertheless one that must be kept in mind. If it happens early in your gambling or at a time when your finances are low, it's enough to knock you out of the gambling picture completely.

Betting on the Odds for the maximum allowed by the casino, when considered together with your line bets, reduces the over-all gambling cost to you when it is expressed as a percentage of the total amount you risk. I don't believe in combining the line bets and the bets on the Odds for any composite statistics that may result, however, and I think you'll be better off if you regard the line bets just for what they are, and the bets on the Odds independently.

Bets on the Odds, in themselves, literally form a "game within a game" in Craps.

You can win even when you lose!

This phenomenon can take place in several different ways when you bet on the Odds. If your losses are mostly on the come-out while a corresponding or greater number of wins are made while betting for or against the point at the proper odds, you can come out ahead thanks to those

Odds bets, while showing no gain, or even a loss, on your line bets.

You can expect to win about 49.3 percent of your line bets. Gamblers who play the front line exclusively can win less often and still make a profit through betting on the Odds. If you're playing for single odds, your wins on these will be for a greater amount than your wins on the line bets, while the losses on both will be about the same, or you may even show lower losses on your bets on the Odds than on your line bets.

The expectation of winning front-line bets after the come-out on them, with all points considered as a group, is 40 percent. You already have the advantage of a ratio of 2 to 1 in your favor for winning instead of losing on the come-out, so if you can guess right at least two fifths of the time on front-line bets involving a point, you have a good chance to do better than break even.

You don't need much luck to swing the balance in your favor. This ability to sometimes convert no gains or small losses on the line into a net gain on your total gambling, by betting on the Odds, may make possible your favorable showing at Craps over a very long period of time. One particular winning bet out of hundreds of bets that you make in the course of a gambling session could be the one that pays all your gambling costs.

The opportunities you enjoy when you bet on the Odds can be compared to playing baseball where the opposition lets your team start off each inning at bat by giving the first batter a base on balls. Double odds would be like your first two batters getting walks. If your team's batting is poor and all your side can do is strike out or hit pop flies or weak infield bounders, those free base runners will do you no good. They might even be to your detriment because they increase the possibility of hitting into easy force-outs or double plays. On the other hand, if your batters can slam out base hits with men on the bases, when those hits really count, your team will score more runs than if you didn't have the free runners on bases to begin with. Your wins on your line bets after the come-out are what carry the additional gains on the Odds along with them.

If you ever have the rare pleasure of watching really serious, intelligent Crap players in action, you'll observe that the pattern of betting they follow is not complicated. As a rule they'll make line bets only and back up those bets whenever possible for the maximum amounts that they can bet on the Odds. If they win a little on the line they'll usually win a lot more on the Odds. Take a tip. Do the same.

CHAPTER 7

ROULETTE

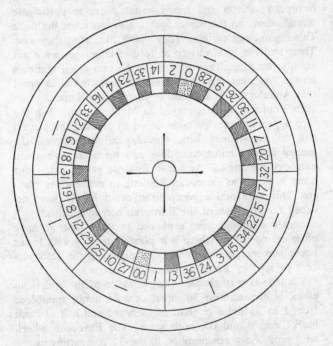

When you think of gambling you automatically have Roulette in mind because it's the most popularized and most widespread of all the casino gambling games. You'll find Roulette in all countries where legal gambling casinos exist. In illegal gambling, which also exists all over the world, Roulette assumes a more important role than it does in the

United States, where Craps easily tops it in popularity. "The Man Who Broke the Bank at Monte Carlo," in fictional literature and popular song, did more to advertise Roulette than all the planned publicity paid for by gambling interests.

Roulette briefly attracted international attention during the 1960 Winter Olympic Games held at Squaw Valley. European athletes and sports writers, here to participate in and report on the winter sports, also looked at the Lake Tahoe gambling casinos. They didn't like what they saw. Their remarks in a variety of foreign languages were not exactly flattering. They pointed to the two green numbers on the American Roulette wheel as incontrovertible proof that Americans are a nation of merciless robbers.

In Roulette, as it is played in Monte Carlo, when the zero appears the casino takes only half of what the players risk on even-money bets. Nevada casinos take all the money under similar conditions and there are two green numbers, making the American Roulette game nearly four times as costly as European Roulette to even-money players. This unfavorable comparison could hardly have escaped the attention of the European correspondents.

Someone should have explained to them that we have other casino games where it is possible to play with lower house percentages on even-money bets than the 1.35 percent enjoyed by Roulette players in Europe.

Roulette is very simple. The perimeter of the American wheel is divided into 38 equal compartments, numbered from 1 to 36 inclusive (half of them red and half of them black) and 0 and 00, both green. The European wheel, with only one green number, 0, has 37 compartments.

A tourneur spins the wheel in one direction while throwing a small ivory ball so it revolves inside the bowl in the opposite direction. As the ball loses speed it falls lower into the bowl until it hits an obstruction and then makes contact with the wheel. It finally becomes trapped in the compartment which identifies the winning number.

In Craps all bets have to be made before the shooter throws the dice. Roulette allows you to make bets anytime before the ball stops revolving inside the bowl. The extra time gamblers have for making their bets works to the pleasure of both the gamblers and the casino. The house, as expected, wants all the action possible.

Roulette inspires confidence in gambling honesty. The wheel and the ball rotating in opposing directions makes it impossible for the tourneur to favor any preselected result. The customers are not allowed to handle the equipment. Finally, the house's margin of profit is no well-guarded secret as in Blackjack or Keno. It is represented by the green number or numbers and you can bet on these as well as on any of the others. Any rigging of the wheel, if it were done, would be toward making the green numbers appear more often. Your ability to bet on them should completely allay any fears about this.

Gamblers are quick to notice any aberrations in the behavior of the Roulette wheel. The leisurely pace and relatively long time between spins prompt many Roulette players to keep a record of the winning numbers. If certain numbers or groups consistently win more often than they should, alert gamblers can clean up handsomely by betting on those numbers.

The casinos know this too and it all helps to guarantee that the wheel is honest. A crooked wheel is easily detected. Inspectors make periodic tests of the balance of the wheels. The compartments for each number and the partitions between them are measured with micrometer calipers. Any bending of the partitions or changes in their heights could favor certain numbers at the expense of other numbers. An inspector, finding a Roulette wheel rigged in this manner, could cause the gambling casino to be closed down completely. So far no complaints of this type have been made in Nevada.

Some of the Nevada casinos publicly post a record of how many times each number has come up during the pre-

vious 24-hour measurement period. If certain numbers be-
have in an eccentric pattern, away off from average expectations, it will promote a flurry of betting on those numbers
by "system" players. Unlike Craps, where an estimated 80
to 90 percent of the line bets are made on the front line,
Roulette players show no decided preference one way or
the other on the even-money bets, and with bets about the
same on red and black, for example, any gains made by the
backers of one color will be largely at the expense of those
who bet on the other.

The game as played in the United States is noticeably
different from the European game in its conduct. In Nevada
the tourneur is dispensed with and the croupier spins the
wheel, throws the ball, announces the winning number,
and proceeds to collect and pay off bets. A rake is not
used in the American game. A second employee is only
required when the table is crowded and betting is heavy.
Then an assistant helps with counting and piling chips.

Roulette is usually played with chips supplied at the layout. The player determines the value of the chips he uses.
Chips are sold in stacks of 20, and with this as the minimum sold you can buy into the game for as little as $1
where the minimum bet is 5 cents. At tables with a 10-cent
minimum a stack costs you $2. You can place a higher
unit value on them yourself, if you prefer, and if you paid
$5 for that same stack of 20 chips they would be worth
25 cents each.

The casino uses small round markers with the numbers
5, 10, 20, 25, 50, 100, 500, or 1000 to denote that a stack
of 20 chips of the color you're using is worth that many
dollars if the stack is valued at more than the minimum.
Stack values for any intermediate amount can be designated by using two or more markers to arrive at that figure.
Casinos carry six or seven colors of chips at a layout, and
200 or 300 of each color.

If your luck is good and you find yourself in possession
of most of the chips of the color you play with, you can

have them revalued by turning some of them in so the ones you still have on hand are individually worth more. Let's say you bought 50 chips for $5, worth 10 cents each, and won $20 worth in your playing, so you now have 250 chips and the house has only 50 of the same color. In order to achieve a more convenient balance to both the player and the house, 200 of the chips can be turned in to the croupier. The 50 you still have on hand are worth as much as the 250 you just had, and the $10 marker placed on your color shows that these chips are now worth $10 a stack, or 50 cents each.

"Breaking the bank" does not mean that you have caused the casino to become insolvent, but that you have cornered the assets of the casino ordinarily carried at the layout where you're playing. With 300 chips raised to their maximum value of $1000 a stack or $50 each, you'll have to win $15,000, or, to put it more correctly, raise what you started with up to that figure. If you "break the bank" on your color, it does not mean that the casino is finished. It can bring in more chips of that color from one of the other layouts, or it can assign you another color if not used by other players at your table. The actual cash represented by your chips won't be in sight, but on your announced intention of cashing them in, arrangements will be made to pay you off in currency, or, if you prefer, with the casino's check for the required amount.

Betting in Roulette is done on single numbers or on combinations of two, three, four, five, six, twelve or eighteen numbers. The bets and the payoffs are as follows:

Straight plays on a single number pay 35 to 1.

Split plays are on two adjacent numbers on the layout. You put your bet on the line between the two numbers. If either wins, the house pays you 17 to 1.

Street plays are placed on the outside line to bet on the three numbers across, paying 11 to 1 if any of the three appears.

Quarter or corner plays are on four numbers making a

square. You place your bet on the intersecting lines. If one of the four numbers comes up, you're paid 8 to 1.

The House Special on the American layout covers five numbers: 0, 00, 1, 2, and 3. You place your bet as a line play at the junction of 0 and 1 on the outside line, covering the two streets 0—00 and 1—2—3. The 0—00 is not a regular street like any of the others with three numbers across, but when combined with the street 1—2—3, the two combinations covered by one bet form the House Special. The payoff is 6 to 1. You really should be collecting 6.2 to 1 here, so instead of making the House Special bet in one lump, divide it into five equal parts and cover each of the numbers separately as a straight play. This will save you from being one betting unit short if you win. A five-chip bet on the House Special wins you 30 chips. With one chip bet straight on each of the numbers 0, 00, 1, 2, and 3, you win 35 chips on your winning number, lose the four chips on the other numbers, and have a net gain of 31 chips.

Line plays cover six numbers. You make your bet on the outside line at the intersection between two streets. You win 5 to 1.

Column plays are on the twelve numbers in either of the three columns headed by 1, 2, or 3. Your bet goes in the designated box at the end of the layout farthest from the wheel. The payoff is 2 to 1.

Dozens, separated as 1st 12, 2nd 12, and 3rd 12, also pay 2 to 1. You make your bet in the box describing the dozen you have chosen.

A bet on the line separating the 2nd and 3rd dozens is not a bet on those dozens, as it appears, but a split play covering 0 and 00. It can be placed there by players so far removed from the head of the layout that they can't reach all the way up to the green numbers. On the European layout having only one green number, the 0, a bet in this position is a straight play on that number.

The minimum limit refers to the lowest value possible for a bet on the numbered part of the layout, either with a chip or a coin of that value. Most Nevada Roulette wheels have a 10-cent minimum limit, although in downtown Reno and Las Vegas some can be found where you can play for only a nickel.

The dozens, columns, and even-money bets, generally called "Outside Bets" because they're not made on the numbered part of the layout, require a minimum bet of five times the table minimum. Thus, even-money bets have to be made for at least 50 cents in cash or chips where the advertised table minimum is 10 cents.

The maximum limit is the highest amount that the casino will pay off on any bet. If it's $1000, you can bet up to that much on an even-money bet, $500 on dozens or columns that pay 2 to 1, $200 on line plays paying 5 to 1, and so forth. An exception is made for straight plays. You can bet $30 on a single number, winning 35 to 1, or a payoff of $1050.

A familiar sight for a long time in one of the Reno casinos was a little silver-haired lady about seventy years old, playing Roulette with the casino's regular $5 chips. She scattered them all over the layout with reckless abandon, covered each number with 1 to 10 chips and always had about $500 in action. After each spin the croupier shoved 35 or more $5 chips her way. It certainly looked attractive to see a game with a "winner" every time.

The house earned about $25 on her betting on every spin. At an estimated rate of a spin a minute, that's $1500 an hour. When you saw this same player going strong for hours at a stretch every time you visited this casino, you formed the impression that she was no ordinary person. The house prides itself on not employing shills. No sane individual would be paying $25 a minute all day long just to be entertained at a gambling table. Those watching could only conclude that she was either a relative or a close personal friend of one of the owners. Who else could afford to spend $12,000 daily in gambling costs and keep it up day after day? The speculators were not wrong. It turned out that one of the owners of the casino was paying her $25 a day out of his own pocket for playing there with chips belonging to the house.

The average earnings by the casino, when expressed either as a fraction or a percentage, are constant. On the American wheel they average $1/19$ of all the money wagered on the table. The margin in favor of the house is $5 5/19$ percent. On European wheels used in Nevada the house earns $1/37$ of the total wagered, or a house percentage of $2 26/37$.

European wheels, when they were first introduced into Nevada, used to be located in upstairs or back rooms, while American wheels dominated the main floor and the more accessible locations. Now the European wheels are coming out into the open, and some casinos use them exclusively. The American wheel is sometimes temporarily converted to function as a European wheel by a sign stating that the house won't collect on 00, but casinos have found that they lose action in such an arrangement and that it's better to replace the wheel with one having 37 compartments and block out the 00 from the layout. Thanks to the intense competition which is a feature of legal gambling in Nevada, you can expect to see more of the European wheels in the future.

If you care to play Roulette, it pays to look for or inquire about the European wheels for the same reason that it pays you to shop and compare prices on any other merchandise or service you pay for. You can cut playing costs nearly in half by playing at a European wheel instead of an American one.

Roulette is the favored game in Europe because its house percentage of 2.7 (reduced to 1.35 on even-money bets) costs less to players than some of the other European casino games. In the United States, Roulette is at a relative disadvantage. Shopping and comparing costs, which is done by all serious gamblers, leads most of them to find Craps a more attractive game. Playing Craps with any skill in your management, principally a matter of sticking to line bets and betting on the Odds whenever possible, and avoiding the sucker bets, reduces the house percentage, or the cost of your gambling, to only a small fraction of what it is in Roulette.

For bets that pay off even money, Roulette is more expensive than line bets in Craps, but there is one comparison in which Roulette is favored. In Craps any proposition with a probability of 1 chance in 36 that you'll win pays off either 30 to 1 or 29 to 1. By making a straight play in Roulette, one chance of success in either 37 or 38, the

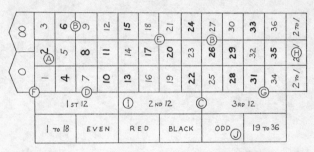

Key to color of single numbers: 0 and 00—green; lightface type—red; boldface type—black

A. Straight play	single number	pays 35 to 1
B. Split play	two adjoining numbers	17 to 1
C. Optional location for split play on 0 and 00		
D. Street play	three numbers in row across	11 to 1
E. Quarter play	four numbers making a square	8 to 1
F. House Special	0, 00, 1, 2, and 3	6 to 1
G. Line play	six numbers in two adjoining streets	5 to 1
H. Column play	twelve numbers in the column	2 to 1
I. Dozen play	twelve numbers in dozen marked in box for the bet	2 to 1
J. Even-money play	group of eighteen numbers as marked in box for the bet	1 to 1

payoff is 35 to 1. Therefore, if you're tempted to put your money on "snake eyes" or "box cars," don't! Bet on a single number in Roulette instead.

Since most of the psychic satisfaction in Roulette comes from getting the maximum payoff of 35 to 1 on a straight play, my recommendation is that, if you play, it should be for minimum amounts on that basis.

For bets that pay off even money you'll do better in Faro, Blackjack, or in the flat bets in Craps.

CHAPTER 8

KENO

PLAY KENO
YOU CAN WIN
$25,000

1	2	3	4	5	6	7	8	9	10
11	12	13	14	15	16	17	18	19	20
21	22	23	24	25	26	27	28	29	30
31	32	33	34	35	36	37	38	39	40

41	42	43	44	45	46	47	48	49	50
51	52	53	54	55	56	57	58	59	60
61	62	63	64	65	66	67	68	69	70
71	72	73	74	75	76	77	78	79	80

Keno card

This book is primarily devoted to Craps because it's my belief that, of all the gambling games you can play in Nevada, Craps offers the most continuous excitement and the best chance to make that fun profitable to yourself. This belief is shared by all who play or observe the games in Nevada with any regularity.

You'll better appreciate Craps when you compare this game with some of the others. Three of them have been chosen for a study in this book because they can easily be compared to Craps: at its lowest cost, its highest cost, and somewhere in between.

The house percentage on your various primary bets in Craps ranges from $1\frac{31}{77}$ up to $20\frac{5}{6}$.

Keno compares to the high-cost bets in Craps. Its inclusion here fills a void in current literature on gambling. Even the books which claim to describe all the casino games do not fully or accurately portray Keno. Few players know either the house percentages or the probabilities of getting any selected score. I feel I am correct in stating that the majority of casino employees, including those directly employed in the game, don't know any more about it than the players.

Your chances of success at Keno are explained in this chapter, and in the Appendix all of the straight Keno tickets from one up to fifteen spots are described in greater detail.

Keno is one of the most popular games in Nevada. Introduced into this country by Chinese laborers imported for railroad construction a century ago, the "Chinese Lottery" of the nineteenth century remains virtually unchanged except for its name and the adaptation of modern mechanical and electronic equipment to its operation.

The player marks anywhere from one up to fifteen spots on a ticket containing 80 numbers. If you're too tired or too lazy to do this yourself, some casinos have premarked tickets in a "grab bag" where you merely pay the price for your ticket and then reach in and pull one out.

Twenty numbered plastic balls are selected at random by the casino from a group of 80. The latest improvement is a transparent cage in which the balls are kept constantly in motion in a current of air. Twenty are removed by suction, one at a time, without being touched by human hands. This operation is performed in plain sight of the players and guarantees that there is no force other than the pure laws of chance governing which numbers are chosen.

If the numbers on some of the spots marked by the player agree with those on the balls selected in the drawing, the player may win amounts varying with the type of ticket he has, the number of spots marked, the price paid for it, his score of "hits," and the advertised rate of payoff for that score. The results of each drawing are flashed on an elaborate electrical scoreboard and announced over a public address system. Stencils with the 20 selected numbers are cut out and, by placing one over your copy of your ticket, you can instantly tell how many spots you hit. The other factors will determine whether you're in the money, and if so, for how much.

The game is designed to pay out only 80 percent of the money it takes in. This makes Keno comparable with the worst of the sucker bets in Craps. In spite of this steep price, Keno has something that serves to keep it high in popularity with the gamblers.

While it is not exactly a lottery in the way it functions or the way payoffs are distributed, it has one of the attractive features of a lottery: the lure of the big payoff. The gambler's chance of getting a perfect score—for example, nine out of nine spots—is a very remote one that becomes still more microscopic with each additional spot marked on the ticket. Probabilities of only one chance out of millions or even billions do not discourage the gamblers. They are inveterate optimists.

Payoffs for getting less than perfect scores make the high cost of playing palatable to the gamblers. Each small win or near miss, or someone else's success, encourages them to try again. *If* they only had marked a row of spots in this column instead of that one, how different things might have been! The return of about 80 percent of the money to the players means that many do get their money back or make small gains, and an occasional big-money payoff to one brightens the hopes of all. Your chance was

as good as the other fellow's. But for the unfortunate accident of marking the wrong spots, that big payoff might
have been yours. If you didn't make it this time, maybe
you will on the next drawing.

Whether you win or lose, there is one thing certain about
Keno. It provides a lot of suspense to those who play it.

The biggest complaint I have against Keno is that there's
a limit on the amount any casino will pay off to all players
combined having winning tickets on a drawing, while there
is no limit on the number or the price of the tickets sold.

Most casinos have a limit of $25,000 in total payoffs in
one game, although in some it is as low as $10,000. If two
different players each hit a $25,000 winner in the same
drawing, they'll have to share that amount on terms certain
to be disliked by both of them. Each holder of a winning
ticket, no matter what the amount, expects to get paid off
at the advertised rate for his score regardless of what luck
any other players might have had on the same drawing.
While a large percentage of a big payoff must be earmarked
for income taxes by the recipient, anything taken off the
top by other than government tax authorities is going to be
seriously resented. My statistical studies on Keno show that
the casinos could afford to pay off the full advertised payoff for each ticket, even if a dozen different players each
gets a $25,000 winner in one drawing or if one player holds
that many tickets with each one winning $25,000.

The mathematical procedure for computing your
chances of getting into the money and the price you pay
for playing is not a complicated one.

On a one-spot ticket the chance that your selected spot
will be one of the 20 (out of 80) picked in the drawing is
exactly that, $20/80$, or one fourth. The casino pays you
3.20 for 1, meaning that you risked one betting unit (the
price of your ticket) to win 2.20 more. You should have
won three at correct odds, and the house percentage is 20.

This bite is such an expensive one that for all practical

purposes I would be justified in telling you that Keno, as now conducted, is only for suckers.

In spite of that, any attempt to discourage gamblers by quoting correct odds or house percentages is probably useless, and Keno will continue to be popular on account of the infinitesimally small chance you have of getting the maximum payoff.

If you believe in miracles it *is* possible to win $25,000 for 50 cents, although the odds are overwhelmingly against it.

Hitting fourteen out of fourteen spots is a probability of 1 chance in 38,910,016,282. Fourteen hits on a fifteen-spot ticket also pays $25,000 for 50 cents. The probability is 1 in 2,853,401,194. The perfect fifteen-spot ticket is the goal of all players who mark such a ticket. You have 1 chance in 428,010,179,098.

If you're still interested in Keno we'll go further. Your chance of getting both spots on a two-spot ticket and winning is $\frac{20 \times 19}{80 \times 79}$ or $\frac{380}{6320}$ or $\frac{1}{16.63}$.

After your first spot has scored, there are 79 more left in the group. Of them, 19 can result in an additional hit and 60 are sure losers.

The casino pays you 13 for 1. You should have received 16.63 at correct odds for your risk. Eighty percent of that is 13.30, so the payoff closely follows the 80-percent formula but is a trifle short. You have been clipped for the breakage, which is the reluctance of the house to recognize terminal digits or decimals in making payoffs. You'll find this trend general throughout the game, although there are a few notable exceptions.

The formula for figuring probabilities in Keno is simple. Actually there are two ways of doing it. There are some advantages and disadvantages to each, and one can be used as a check on the other. You can first determine the total number of different combinations of so many numbers from the group out of which they're selected. Then you determine the number of possible combinations that include no hit, one hit, two hits, and so forth, up to the full number of spots marked on the ticket. The other way is to directly figure the probability of getting any selected score, then multiply that figure by another figure from a table known as Pascal's Pyramid, which determines the number of possible combinations in that particular stratum.

Both these procedures are a standard part of any elementary course in statistics at the collegiate level.

I will demonstrate both methods on the three-spot ticket, where the figures are not as voluminous as on tickets with a greater number of marked spots.

There are $\frac{80 \times 79 \times 78}{1 \times 2 \times 3}$, or 82,160, different combinations of three things at a time taken from a group of 80.

The four different strata break down as follows:

3 hits: $\frac{20 \times 19 \times 18}{1 \times 2 \times 3}$ =   1140 combinations

2 hits: $\left(\frac{20 \times 19}{1 \times 2}\right)\left(\frac{60}{1}\right)$ = 11,400 combinations

1 hit: $\left(\frac{20}{1}\right)\left(\frac{60 \times 59}{1 \times 2}\right)$ = 35,400 combinations

0 hit: $\frac{60 \times 59 \times 58}{1 \times 2 \times 3}$ = 34,220 combinations

Figuring the percentage of the total that is contained in each stratum is simply a matter of addition and then long division.

Your chance of hitting all three spots on a three-spot ticket can be more directly figured as $\frac{20 \times 19 \times 18}{80 \times 79 \times 78}$, or $\frac{6,840}{492,960}$, which can be reduced to $\frac{1}{72.07}$. The probability can be expressed as 1 chance in 72.07, or as 1.3875+ percent, and the odds against hitting all three spots are 71.07 to 1.

To get two out of three it's $\dfrac{20 \times 19 \times 60}{80 \times 79 \times 78}$, or $\dfrac{22,800}{492,960}$, multiplied by three (because there are three different ways of getting this combination), which equals $\dfrac{68,400}{492,960}$, or $\dfrac{1}{7.207}$.

When we go into three-spot tickets we introduce a variation in the payoff because, instead of paying for perfect scores only, the casino pays something to the ticket holder who hits two out of three. It's 1 for 1 or your money back, hardly anything a gambler will get enthused about, but it's there and deserves attention.

An average of 1.3875 percent of three-spot tickets sold will have hits on all three spots. The advertised rate of payoff is 47 for 1, so the casino can figure to pay out $65.21 (from each $100 taken in) to holders of tickets with perfect scores. Another 13.875 percent of ticket holders will hit two out of three and get their money back. This will cost the casino $13.88 out of each $100 taken in. Together that amounts to $79.09 out of $100. Once again the players were taken for the breakage. After the players who hit two out of three got their money back, those with perfect scores should have received 47.70 for 1 if the formula for returning 80 percent of the money to the players had been strictly adhered to.

To go into complete detail about all of the mathematical procedures affecting payoffs on all of the different Keno tickets would fill a book bigger than this one. Space limitations require skipping everything from here on except for important summaries and comments on a few oddities of special interest. I will discuss straight Keno tickets only because the more complicated tickets hold very little interest for the average gambler.

It becomes clear as we go along that an increasingly larger proportion of the total paid out to players gets diverted from the maximum payoff onto other scores as more possibilities are added, with each additional spot marked, for payoffs to players who get less than perfect scores. I refer you to the Appendix for this vital information.

The seven-spot ticket in almost all casinos is unique in that it pays money back to players who hit no spots out of seven. These amount to slightly over 12 percent of the total. In some casinos the tickets pay off something on all scores from no hits up to seven hits, but when you go into details about the total payoffs they run pretty close to 79 percent of what is taken in, and you're not getting anything for nothing.

The thing that attracts you to the Keno game and what you're no doubt most interested in is the maximum payoff for the perfect score, and your chance of marking a perfect ticket. You'll come to some definite conclusions as you digest this information and the true picture of Keno unfolds itself.

At the lower levels up to and including five spots, Keno runs a poor second to parlayed line bets in Craps with almost identical risks. Your chance of hitting three spots out of three in Keno is 1 in slightly over 72, for which the casino pays you 47 for 1. Nearly the same risk, trying to make six consecutive passes in Craps, offers you 1 chance of success in 70 and pays off 64 for 1 on your parlayed bets.

A five-spot Keno ticket, with your probability for a perfect score being 1 chance in 1550+, pays you 360 for 1 on this score. Some casinos pay only 332 for 1. You can try for 10 straight passes in Craps, a probability of 1 in 1181 that you'll make it, and the reward is 1024 for 1—almost three times as much as the maximum payoff on the five-spot Keno ticket on which you're bucking a risk over 30 percent greater.

As the number of spots marked on a Keno ticket increases, so does the disparity between the maximum payoff ratio on that ticket and your probability of getting it.

Casino walls are prominently decorated with Keno tickets that have won big money in the past. It's an effective come-on for advertising the game. In my opinion it proves nothing except that the casinos are doing an enormous volume of business!

My personal recommendation about Keno is not a good one. If your gambling blood demands a few tries at getting rich quick, whatever the cost or the odds against you, just be sensible about it and don't go overboard chasing rainbows. Keep your ticket purchases low in amount so that the maximum advertised payoff is below the casino's aggregate payoff limit. An expenditure of about $5 on 10 tickets for 50 cents each or 9 tickets for 55 cents each brings you

ANALYSIS OF PERFECT KENO TICKETS

Spot sequence	Your chance of a hit on this spot if you have no previous failures		Cumulative probability of success on this and previous spots— one chance in	Percent of casino's receipts paid out to holders of perfect tickets	On ticket with payoff ratio (to price of ticket)
1st	$20/80$ or	.25000	4.00	80.00	3.2
2nd	$19/79$	.24501	16.63	78.16	13
3rd	$18/78$	.23077	72.07	65.21	47
4th	$17/77$	.22078	326.44	36.15	118
5th	$16/76$	.21053	1,550.57	23.22	360
6th	$15/75$	.20000	7,752.84	15.99	1,240
7th	$14/74$	.18919	40,979.31	3.66	1,500
8th	$13/73$	.17808	230,114.61	1.67	3,840
9th	$12/72$	.16667	1,380,687.65	.467	6,440
10th	$11/71$	.15493	8,911,711.18	.291	25,000
11th	$10/70$	.14286	62,381,978.24	.0401	25,000
12th	$9/69$	.13043	478,261,833.14	.00523	25,000
13th	$8/68$	.11765	4,065,225,581.67	.000394	16,000
14th	$7/67$	.10448	38,910,016,281.67	.000129	50,000
15th	$6/66$	.09091	428,010,179,098.33	.0000117	50,000

the probability that with average luck you'll hit one or two small payoffs and get nearly $4 of your money back.

If one of your tickets is the one in millions and you strike it rich right away for one of the big payoffs, more power to you. Here's wishing you luck. You'll need lots of it.

CHAPTER 9

FARO

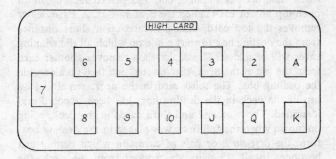

Faro was the most popular gambling game in the cattle-trading towns and mining camps of the West during the nineteenth century. At the peak of the California gold rush excitement the town of Columbia boasted of having 134 Faro Banks. Faro is the name of the game itself and Faro Bank generally refers to the layout on which it is played, a relationship similar to Craps and Crap table with reference to each other. You play Faro at a Faro Bank.

Faro has largely been replaced by Craps and other games of chance that are faster and less complicated.

If you're too young to collect your Social Security retirement benefits and have never been in Nevada, it's an almost sure bet that you've never seen a real live Faro game in action. Even those who have recently visited Nevada may not have seen or heard of the Faro game. Few amateur gamblers are acquainted with it and the fact that it is still being played. The almost total absence of any reliable printed literature about Faro is a factor in its not being better known today.

Westerns which are shown on television frequently contain scenes in gambling halls, with Faro the center of attention. You'll enjoy these television shows much better when you understand exactly what is going on.

Faro is played with a standard 52-card deck of playing cards. The deck is shuffled, cut, and placed face up in an open-top box or cage called the *dealing box*. A Faro dealer removes the top card, laying it face up a short distance from the dealing box to start a pile on which all the winning cards will be added. The dealer then removes another card from the top of the deck, placing that one face up alongside the dealing box. The third card in the deck, remaining on top of the deck in the dealing box, has been exposed and identified. Those second and third cards in the deck, being unknown when the full deck was placed in the dealing box, form the first *turn*, or pair of cards on which betting can be done. In all, 25 pairs are worked from the deck; the final card, because it can't be paired with another, is discarded and does not directly figure in the betting.

In the gambling language applicable to Faro, the card that remains in the dealing box following the action on each turn is the *winner* and the first active card withdrawn from the dealing box falling alongside it is the *loser*, just as in Craps you have almost similar terms referring to the decision on the shooter's roll when expressed from the standpoint of the front line. In Faro it's the position the card is in when it appears following the action on the turn, rather than its value or denomination, that makes it the winner or loser.

Special names are given to the top and bottom cards in the deck, both of which are discarded. The first discard is the *soda* and the final one the *hock*, which is sometimes spelled *hoc*. A common nineteenth-century slang expression, "from soda to hock," meant everything from beginning to end or, as we would say it today, "from A to Z."

The layout on which the betting is done consists of one card of each denomination in the deck, or an enlarged replica of that card, on a flat surface. The spades suit is usually represented.

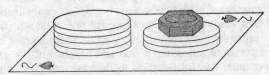

Left—This bet is on the denomination to win.
Right—This bet is on the denomination to lose.

In ordinary Faro betting your wager is that the denomination on which you're betting will either be a winner or a loser when it appears. A straight bet on the card means you're betting it will be a winner. *Coppering* your bet (placing a small six-sided black chip on top of it) signifies the opposite intention: that you want the card to be a loser.

You can also bet on *high card,* shown on the layout directly in front of the dealer. A straight bet is on the winner to be a higher denomination than the loser. A coppered bet is for the loser to be the high card. Aces count as the lowest value in the deck. The high-card bet provides action on every turn.

The house's advantage lies in the probability that both cards in a turn will be the same denomination. That situation, called a *split,* is really a win and a loss for the player at the same time and should be a stand-off, but the house keeps half of your bet.

If the denomination on which you have bet doesn't appear in the first turn after you have made your bet, the same process is repeated. The winner of the turn just completed is removed from the dealing box and placed on the pile farthest away from it. The next card appearing is also removed from the dealing box and placed on top of the pile alongside it, becoming the loser in the turn currently being worked. The winner remains exposed in the dealing box. This action results in the exposure of the two previously unknown cards and a new chance to either win or lose your bet.

A *case keeper,* or scorer, manipulates an abacus-type counting board with beads, showing which denominations and how many of them have already been removed from the dealing box or exposed on top of it. This makes it easy for a player to follow the action and progress of the game at any time. Careful attention to the case and the position of the beads is essential if you want to play Faro to your best advantage.

Beads representing the denominations of the cards are moved toward the outer edge of the case as each card is removed from the dealing box or exposed as the top card in the deck remaining within the dealing box. A bead pushed against the outer edge of the case or touching the bead of that denomination previously worked designates a loser. A space separating the bead from the outer edge of the case or the bead of the denomination previously worked means a winner.

A coppering chip placed on one of the denominations pictured on the case identifies the soda card. The bead representing the soda is pushed out to the winner position.

Faro has a strong appeal to gamblers who like to follow a "system." The system can be anything that the player devises for his guidance and gambling pleasure, but one of the most common of those followed in Faro is in betting that all four cards of a certain denomination will fall the same way, as all winners or all losers. A player noticing the trend established by the first two cards of a denomination falling the same way will, knowing that the house percentage is relatively low, bet on that card to win or lose for the third time. If it goes the same way three times, there is no house percentage on the next bet on that card, and a player following this system is more likely than not to let his money ride, parlaying his bets to win as much as

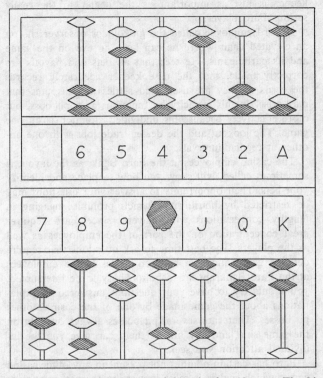

The case, showing position of the beads after 10 turns. The 21
cards have been recorded in the following order:

10	6	J	8	7	A	7	K	3	8	8	3	2	7	5	A	5	J	7	10	4
Soda	Loser	Winner	L	W	L	W	L	W	L	W	L	W	L	W	L	W	L	W	L	W

The fifth turn was a split.

possible on a series of correct guesses on them. The case keeper is just as important as the dealer to the really serious Faro player.

A third employee called the *lookout* or observer sits on an elevated chair where he can keep an eye on the game and its participants. He sees that all bets and payoffs are correctly made, that the case keeper accurately records the cards as they are used, and settles any disputes that may arise. In this capacity he functions as a pit boss, but more effectively because his undivided attention is on one game. The lookout and the dealer trade jobs with one another at regular intervals.

The casino employees at the Faro Bank, as the layout is sometimes called, will show you how to place and identify your bets. Their opportunity to answer your questions may be restricted by house rules which prohibit engaging in lengthy conversations with players, since Faro requires great concentration on the part of the employees as well as the players. The best time to ask questions that require detailed explanations is between deals. If the employees at the Faro Bank appear to be too busy to be interrupted, you should try to have your questions answered or explanations about the game made by one of the casino's other pit bosses. There are several pit bosses always on duty on the same shift and any one of them can give you the individual attention you seek.

Faro has certain oddities not present in any other casino game, which makes it most interesting to mathematicians and to students of gambling generally. There is no house percentage for the game as a whole, and the house's advantage changes with each new turn being worked. The probability of both cards in a turn being the same denomination gets less as one or more of that denomination have been used. There will be fewer of the same denomination remaining in the yet unworked portion of the deck. The probability of a split becomes greater as each turn is worked without that denomination appearing because fewer unknown cards remain in the balance of the deck from which a matching pair can be drawn.

Some gamblers ignore the mechanics of the game altogether and assume that because the probability that any card drawn from a deck of 52 will be followed by another of the same denomination is 1 in 17, and the house keeps half your bet when there's a split, the house's advantage is $\frac{1}{34}$ of the gross betting, or a percentage of 2.94.

That figure, if the reasoning were valid, could only be applied to the high-card bet and would not be effective when the remaining cards in the deal are all case cards. On the regular even-money bets on any specified denomination to win or lose, the house's advantage is not an across-the-board matter as in Roulette, but is only exercised against the bets on the denomination of the split as far as single bets are concerned. Assuming bets of equal amounts on all the cards, it is closer to reality to say that the house's average earnings on regular even-money betting are $\frac{1}{442}$ of the gross betting. There is no guarantee that the house will earn this very small proportion, or anything at all. In Roulette, when one of the house numbers (the 0 or 00) appears, the house always earns *something* by collecting the bets made on all other numbers or combinations. A split can and often does occur in Faro when there is no money being bet on that card, and half of nothing is, of course, still nothing.

As already stated, no single house-percentage figure can be given for the whole game. The house percentage varies at each stage depending on how many of the denomination you're betting on have already been disposed of and how many cards still remain in the unworked portion of the deck inside the dealing box. There are 25 turns being worked and four different levels (none gone, one gone, two gone, and three gone) at which it is possible to place bets on a single card, less three combinations which must be subtracted from the 100 because they can't be made. Special conditions apply to the working of the final turn if you're making a bet that pays off more than even money.

If two or three are gone you couldn't start betting any earlier than the second turn. Those two or three of the same denomination would be either two thirds or all of the first three cards in the deal, with at least one of the cards in the first turn certain to be included.

If none is gone, you couldn't make a bet at that level on the 25th turn. All four of any denomination concentrated at the very end of the deal would take up the hock card and both cards in the final turn, spilling over into the 24th turn where one card of that denomination will be used.

Listing all 97 instances possible for making bets on a single card and computing the probabilities of a split and the house percentage for each gives you a panorama of the game at a glance. You have all this information at the end of this chapter.

The actual earnings by the casino will be in the very low range of house percentages because few if any of the customers will be making any of the high-cost bets. The wisest ones will wait until three cards of any denomination have already been disposed of to get that cost-free gambling which only Faro offers in a primary bet.

You'll see plenty of activity in any Faro game right from the first turn on. Even when the house's advantage is at its greatest (when bets are made on denominations that have all four cards unworked), the deal has to progress to the 14th turn for the house percentage to rise to as much as 1 percent. Bets on "one gone" cards can be made beginning with the first turn when you bet on the denomination of the soda, and no later than the eighth turn you can begin betting on "two gone" cards. Intelligent gamblers, knowing the correct house percentages for each situation, can keep that percentage well below one third of 1 percent at all times when their bets are subject to a split.

Bets can be made on a single card or on certain combinations of two, three, or four cards. You can bet on any number of cards separately if you desire. The bet can be left straight, for a card to win, or coppered, for it to lose. When two or more cards are covered in one bet, the first card on which there is action determines the entire bet. If all the cards in a combination bet are bet to win, or to lose, any two of those cards (of different denominations) in such a combined bet result in a stand-off on your bet if they appear in the same turn. You win on one of the cards and lose on the other one at the same time.

Because of the possibility of splits most betting in Faro is done with an even number of chips. The dealer can, if he has to, reach into a cash drawer and give a player $1.25 in silver for the player's chip worth $2.50, or $2.50 change for a chip worth $5, but this slows up the game and is discouraged as much as possible. The house rules may require you to bet a minimum of two chips, or to bet an even-numbered quantity of them on all bets subject to a split.

In a two-way combination bet, where you bet on one card to win and another to lose, action on one of those cards determines the bet. You either guessed correctly or wrongly on the result. If both denominations appear in the turn it isn't a stand-off, as it is when both are bet in the same direction. Let's say you bet on King to win and Queen to lose. If the King and Queen appear in the same turn in the correct order of your bet you have won your bet on each of them and you get paid off for the double win. If they come in the reverse order you're "whipsawed" and have lost twice. The dealer will collect your bet on the table for your payment of one of those losses. You owe an equal amount to the dealer for your second loss, and that debt must be settled immediately. Two-way combination bets (except when you're calling the turn in the final turn) should never be made unless you have sufficient chips or reserve assets—cash in your pocket—to cover your possible losses.

A bet on a single card is placed directly on that card.

In a bet on a combination of two cards, they can be

either adjacent in the same row, in the same row but separated by another card between them, directly opposed to each other in separate rows, diagonally opposed, or so far apart that the bet has to be handled in a special manner.

Beginners seem to get confused by layout diagrams that show all the possible types of bets in one illustration, so it is best to proceed with examples of bets on a combination of two cards first. We'll take up the other combinations later.

Bets on two cards either adjacent in the same row or directly opposed in separate rows are made in the space between them.

Bets on two cards in the same row, separated by another card between them, are made on the outside corner of one card, pointing toward the other. They can be made on either card except when one of the cards is the 7.

Bets on cards diagonally opposed can be placed *off* the inside corner of one card, pointing toward the other. You can make any size bet in this location with your chips or

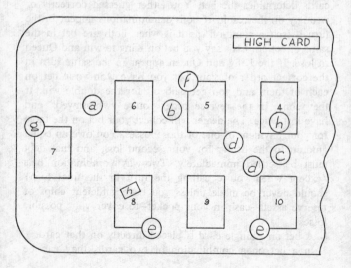

coins in a straight stack. If your bet is made with only one
chip or coin it would have to be here.

a. Bet on 6 and 7.
b. Bet on 6 and 5.
c. Bet on 4 and 10.
d. Bet on 5 and 10.
e. Bet on 8 and 10.
f. Bet on 7 and 5.
g. *Not* a bet on 7 and 5.

> Bets touching any part of the 7 card on the layout
> are single bets on 7 only and do not combine with
> any other cards. The corner of the 7 has no sig-
> nificance. If you want to bet on a combination of
> 7 and 5 you have to make your bet on the outside
> corner of the 5, pointing toward the 7, and not the
> other way around.

h. Bet on 4 and 8, using a marker on the 8.

> The player using a marker establishes its value at
> the time for whatever he announces that value to
> be. In this instance it would be equal to the amount
> bet on the 4. A pair of 4s or a pair of 8s appearing
> in a turn are a split affecting this bet. The house col-
> lects half the bet on the split. The house will pick
> up half the money the player has put on the 4 if the
> split is on 8, which is only covered by the marker.
> If the player loses his bet by unfavorable action on
> the 8, the house will likewise pick up all the player's
> money from the 4. The marker changes in value
> along with any change in the bet to which it is re-
> lated.

It is obvious that only one bet can occupy the off-the-
corner position, but if many players want to make the
same type of bet there are various ways of getting them
all on the layout. The bet on the same two cards can be
made off the inside corner of the second card. Bets can
be piled on top of other bets, and it is not unusual to see
a high stack with bets by several players, each player's bet

identified by the distinctive color or design of the chips he is using. Finally, there is an alternate method of betting on diagonally opposed cards that does not involve the off-the-corner position. A *heeled bet,* with the bottom chip resting flat on one of the cards and the remainder of the chips resting on an edge of that chip and leaning toward the other card in the combination, means the same thing. If space does not allow this, a straight stack on one of the cards and a marker on the other also means the same type of a bet. Both parts of the bet—the bottom chip and the leaning stack resting on it, or the straight stack and the marker associated with it—are coppered if you're betting on either of the diagonally opposed cards to lose.

When two cards are so far separated on the layout that a single combination bet can't be made to cover both of them, then you have to duplicate the bet on the second card, playing both separately but at the same time, or use a marker for this purpose. The dealer knows that your money on one card guarantees your payment to the house if a split or losing action affects your bets.

If a combination bet on two cards, using a marker on one, is not all made in the same direction—that is, when you're betting one card to win and the other to lose—there is a possibility that you can lose both bets simultaneously. The dealer will accept your marker as an "I.O.U." only when he is satisfied that your credit is good for that amount and that you can meet your obligations.

A heeled bet in opposite directions on two cards, betting one to win and the other to lose, is called a heel-and-toe bet. It can be made at any time but is most likely to be seen on the calling of the final turn, where it can assume spectacular proportions due to the amount of chips piled up.

The single coppered chip that rests solidly on the layout is either touching or pointing to the loser. The pile comprising the remainder of the bet leans toward the winner. If a heel-and-toe bet is between two adjacent or opposite cards it need not touch either card. The position of the coppered bottom chip and the direction in which the rest of them are leaning will instantly identify the winner and the loser.

A HEEL-AND-TOE BET

The top pile leans toward the winner; the coppered chip touches or points to the loser.

Bets on a combination of any three cards forming a triangle on the layout are placed *on* the inside corner of the angle card. A bet in this position on the Ace would also include the 2 and the King. If the bet isn't touching the angle card it could be interpreted as a two-card combination bet including the card diagonally opposite. This might lead to some disagreements between the players and the house on action affecting any of the cards. It is therefore important that when you want your bet to be *on* the corner it should be substantially on it, at least up to the center of the chip, and not on the borderline, where a slight accidental push by the dealer or another player could knock it off the card entirely and change the character of your bet.

When three cards in a combination bet are all in line in the same row, with the 7 included if it is one of the three, the bet can be placed *off* from the outside edge of the center card.

There is no rigidly specified manner for making the combination bet on 6, 7, and 8. The angle corner of the 6 or 8 could not be used. It could be either off the outside edge of the 7, or in the space bounded by the three cards, depending on how the house prefers to have it. It is best to ask the dealer for instructions on making this bet.

A bet on four cards forming a square is placed in the center of the space separating them. The 7 card could not be included in such a bet.

In betting on combinations of three or four cards, all of the betting has to be one way, any of them to win or any of them to lose.

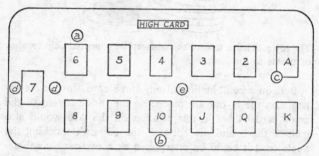

(a.) Bet on 5, 6, and 7. (b.) Bet on 9, 10, and Jack. (c.) Bet on 2, Ace, and King. (d.) Bet on 6, 7, and 8 (subject to house rules). (e.) Bet on 3, 4, 10, and Jack.

Faro reaches its climax of excitement in the betting on the 25th, or final, turn.

When the last three cards in the dealing box, as indicated by the case, include a pair of the same denomination, you have what is known as a *cat-hop*.

On the regular cat-hop (a pair and one case card of a different denomination) you can call the turn for the 2 to 1 payoff by the house if your guess is correct, and this provides most of the excitement and action. You can also make the even-money bet on the case card to win or lose.

Calling the turn in the cat-hop is made in a special manner. You string the bet (spread it out) from the pair toward the case card, from the case card toward the pair, or from the pair toward the outside.

The bottom chip in a strung bet indicates that the card it touches or points to has been selected to be the first active card out of the dealing box in the final turn, or the loser. A strung bet in calling the turn in the cat-hop does not have to have part of it coppered as in making a heel-and-toe bet, because the direction your bet is in already indicates your choice. Stringing the bet from the case card toward the pair means you're betting that the case card will be the loser. From the pair toward the case card is a bet on the case card to win, and from the pair toward the outside is a bet that the pair will form both the cards in the turn and the case card will be, by elimination, the hock. This covers the three possible choices.

It's always a good idea to announce your bet to the dealer when you make it. The dealer will look it over and correct any error you may have made in handling it if you didn't get it quite right.

When a bet is made with only one chip or coin having value, it can also be strung out like a bet composed of several units. You put a coppering chip down first on the loser, then your chip or coin having value on top of it, and another coppering chip on top of that. Your bet, sandwiched between the two coppering chips, can now be handled the same as three chips or coins, and you string them in the desired direction.

A rare situation occurs, once in 425 deals on the average, where the last three cards in the dealing box are all the same denomination. When the case shows this, the dealer will look for the one card of that denomination already used. The case will indicate whether it's in the pile of winners or losers. Its color, whether black or red, establishes that there is one more card of that color and two of the other color in the dealing box.

Betting in this situation is confined to the case card. The card on the layout represents that case card, be it black or red. You can make the even-money case bet for that odd-colored card to win or lose, with no action if it doesn't show up in the turn. If you call the turn for the 2 to 1 payoff, you're also betting on your choice that the case card will win or lose, but you lose the bet if it doesn't come out exactly that way. Thus, in your bet that the case card will win, if you call it for the 2 to 1 payoff, you lose if the case card is the loser or the hock. You should announce such a bet to the dealer and he'll place it for you correctly.

A high-card bet is not recommended when there's a regular cat-hop. Out of the three possible positions the case card can fall in, one of them with the case card as the hock would result in the pair appearing in the turn, and the house taking half your bet on the split results in a house percentage of $16\frac{2}{3}$.

When the denominations of all three cards in the final turn are different, besides the case bet or the high-card bet at even money, you can call the turn and take a chance on naming both the winner and the loser in the turn with a probability of 1 chance in 6 that you'll do it correctly. This bet pays 4 to 1. Getting a payoff of 5 for 1 instead of the 6 for 1 to which correct odds would entitle you means that the house percentage on this particular bet is $16\frac{2}{3}$.

In risk, payoff, and house percentage it is exactly equal to the Any 7 single-throw bet in Craps. Notwithstanding the cost, this is a popular bet with Faro players. Those who are behind in their betting during the deal don't mind risking a little more to try to recover their losses and maybe come out ahead if their luck takes a sudden change for the better, and those whose parlayed bets have put them ahead of the game are not reluctant to use part of their winnings to try for still bigger gains.

Faro has a wider range of house percentages than any

other casino game. For the purpose of comparing Faro to Craps we'll take the case bets and calling the turn in the cat-hop, where there is no percentage favoring the house, and compare them with betting on the Odds in Craps, which is also a no-cost deal for the players.

All Faro bets, except some of those which may be made on the final turn, are for even money. Minimum and maximum limits are usually listed at the layout or on a sign close to it. Where the maximum limit is given in two figures, the lesser refers to case bets and also to calling the turn in the cat-hop. The house has no chance of earning anything on these and imposes a lower limit on them than on other bets where either the possibility of a split or the shortened payoff ratio results in some advantage to the house.

The chips you play with are worth knowing about. As in Roulette, they come in various colors or designs, each of which identifies a particular player's bets. The different colors do not in themselves represent monetary values. Values are set by the players. Stacks of 20 chips in Las Vegas are usually valued at $25, $50, $100, $250, or $500, depending on how much money you want to spend to get into the game and how many chips you want to start playing with. The limits are subject to change by the house and you should ask what they are at the time you play. In Las Vegas, at the customary minimum buy-in price of $25 for a stack of 20 chips, they would be worth $1.25 each. The minimum bet using these chips is for two chips. If you're using the regular house chips, coins, or currency, you have to bet at least $5.

Using the special chips provided at the Faro Bank gives you the same protection that traveler's cheques offer to a tourist. If you use coins or the regular chips that are good anywhere in the casino there's no way you can protect your money except to watch it like a hawk to make sure that another player, by design or accident, doesn't pick it up. If you have a cash bet on any card to win, for example, another player could match your bet, stacking his directly on top of yours, and then copper the stack that includes his money and yours beneath it, to make it look like he's betting all of it on that card to lose. He could move what looks like his bet to another position on the layout and your money would be irrevocably lost to you. I'm not saying that it will happen, but you can eliminate that possibility entirely by using the chips provided at the Faro Bank. I advise that you "buy in" when you play Faro. Your chips can be redeemed for the cash they represent when you decide to quit playing.

Let's say you buy a stack of chips for $25 and happen to have some good luck in your playing and build up your capital to a larger amount. If you have an even number of chips on hand you can turn half of them in to the dealer and he'll place a $50 marker on your color. This has the effect of doubling the value of the chips you still hold, which then are worth $2.50 each. This procedure can be repeated as often as necessary, in reverse if you want more chips of a lower unit value, and it serves to keep the number of chips in circulation at a level convenient to the player and the Faro Bank. The casino may also impose a limit on the value of the chips you have on hand, and if you reach that limit you have to cash them in, then start all over again by buying in for a lower amount.

Few gambling casinos now operate Faro games. In the places where there are Faro Banks they're more a historical reminder of the past than a present-day necessity, being equal in this respect to San Francisco's famous cable cars or to New York City's horse-drawn hansom cabs. The game earns very little for the house and sometimes costs more money to operate than it brings in, and it could easily be eliminated for reasons of economy. It is a credit to the legal gambling business—or to those casinos that make financial sacrifices to keep the game alive—that Faro is still being played. Its existence is a powerful argument against critics of gambling who indiscriminately describe all casino games as sucker traps.

BETS POSSIBLE ON A SINGLE DENOMINATION THROUGHOUT THE DEAL, AND ON CALLING THE TURN IN THE FINAL TURN

TURN SEQUENCE	Number of unworked cards remaining in the dealing box	NONE GONE		ONE GONE		TWO GONE		THREE GONE	
		Probability of a split on denomination of player's bet	Percentage favoring the house	Probability of a split on denomination of player's bet	Percentage favoring the house	Probability of a split on denomination of player's bet	Percentage favoring the house	Probability of a split on denomination of player's bet	Percentage favoring the house
1st	51	12/2550	0.235	6/2550	0.118	a	a	a	a
2nd	49	12/2352	0.255	6/2352	0.128	2/2352	0.0425	0/2352	0.00
3rd	47	12/2162	0.278	6/2162	0.139	2/2162	0.0462	0/2162	0.00
4th	45	12/1980	0.303	6/1980	0.152	2/1980	0.0505	0/1980	0.00
5th	43	12/1806	0.332	6/1806	0.166	2/1806	0.0555	0/1806	0.00
6th	41	12/1640	0.366	6/1640	0.183	2/1640	0.0610	0/1640	0.00
7th	39	12/1482	0.405	6/1482	0.202	2/1482	0.0675	0/1482	0.00
8th	37	12/1332	0.450	6/1332	0.225	2/1332	0.0750	0/1332	0.00
9th	35	12/1190	0.504	6/1190	0.252	2/1190	0.0840	0/1190	0.00
10th	33	12/1056	0.568	6/1056	0.284	2/1056	0.0947	0/1056	0.00
11th	31	12/930	0.645	6/930	0.323	2/930	0.108	0/930	0.00
12th	29	12/812	0.740	6/812	0.370	2/812	0.123	0/812	0.00
13th	27	12/702	0.854	6/702	0.427	2/702	0.142	0/702	0.00
14th	25	12/600	1.00	6/600	0.500	2/600	0.167	0/600	0.00
15th	23	12/506	1.19	6/506	0.593	2/506	0.198	0/506	0.00
16th	21	12/420	1.43	6/420	0.714	2/420	0.238	0/420	0.00
17th	19	12/342	1.75	6/342	0.877	2/342	0.292	0/342	0.00
18th	17	12/272	2.21	6/272	1.10	2/272	0.368	0/272	0.00
19th	15	12/210	2.86	6/210	1.43	2/210	0.476	0/210	0.00
20th	13	12/156	3.86	6/156	1.93	2/156	0.641	0/156	0.00
21st	11	12/110	5.46	6/110	2.73	2/110	0.909	0/110	0.00
22nd	9	12/72	8.33	6/72	4.17	2/72	1.39	0/72	0.00
23rd	7	12/42	14.28	6/42	7.14	2/42	2.38	0/42	0.00
24th	5	12/20	30.00	6/20	15.00	2/20	5.00	0/20	0.00
25th	3	a	a	6/6	0.00[b]	2/6	0.00[c]	0/6	0.00[d]

(a) Bet not physically possible.
(b) Cat-hop. Betting is restricted to the odd-colored card, which is the case card. The zero house percentage is listed to show that the house makes nothing on the cat-hop.
(c) Cat-hop. The odd-ranking card is the case card. Betting can be either on the case card or on the pair.
(d) Calling the turn (naming both the winner and the loser) pays 4 to 1. The house percentage is 16⅔%.

Gamblers, being very impatient souls, have not taken to Faro very well, because the game does require a lot of concentration and patience in waiting for the best time to make bets. The even-money payoffs on the first 24 turns don't appeal to gamblers who are anxious to make their fortunes in one bold lucky stroke, and the low maximum limits fence in those who, in their imaginations, are always thinking big in terms of the maximum possible winnings.

Blackjack, another card game based on even-money betting, is quite popular with gamblers. It is my opinion that the frustration suffered by Faro players lies in their inability to handle the cards being used. Blackjack players can also make decisions affecting, for better or worse, their chances of winning.

Author's recommendation about Faro: the best, if you know how to play it.

CHAPTER 10

BLACKJACK

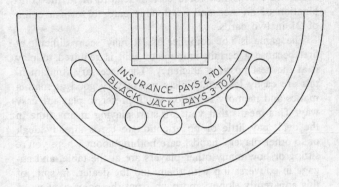

The game of "21," or Blackjack, as it is improperly but more commonly called, is played in all Nevada casinos.

Blackjack, as it is known and played outside of gambling casinos, is a game where the dealer, who is one of the participants, manages the game and banks it against the other players. One of them getting an Ace and a 10 or a picture card has "Black Jack" and becomes the dealer, until he in turn loses the deal to the next player who gets a Black Jack. The dealer can also transfer the deal to another player by auctioning it off to the highest bidder. When played in a "Card Club" or other commercial recreational establishment, the house does not take an active part in the game but collects a fixed fee from all participants or a percentage of the bets from the winners as its price for furnishing the facilities for the game. In a legal gambling casino the dealer is an employee of the house, against which all bets are placed, and the players never take over that function.

Besides the error of common usage where the wrong name has stuck as the one most widely accepted, there are variations in its spelling. In this book I am following a pattern that seems to prevail in most of the literature distributed by Nevada casinos: using *Blackjack* for the game itself and *Black Jack* for a certain feature of it, the combination of an Ace and a 10-value card to form a count of 21 in two cards.

The game is not complicated. It may seem difficult at first because a certain amount of skill is required to play it at the best possible efficiency. The necessary fundamentals are easily learned. Unless you're very good at mathematics and memory retention you'll prefer to play the easy way. This means that you can start playing at any time in the deal, pay little or no attention to cards already dealt or to other players' hands, care nothing about where you're sitting or how many other players are at the table, and engage in conversation with them and the dealer. In spite of this apparently sloppy approach from the point of view of the expert, you can still give a very good account of yourself. The house's most effective weapon against the real expert is shuffling the deck so the players can exercise no advantage from casing the cards as they're used. This won't hurt you when you play the easy way.

The object of the game is to get a count of 21, or as close to it as possible without going over that figure, and do it with a higher count than the dealer, who is also playing his own hand toward that objective. The Ace counts as either 1 or 11, tens and picture cards all have a value of 10, and all other cards are worth their numerical identities.

If both player and dealer have the same count and it's at least 17 and not over 21, it's a draw or stand-off. There are special conditions to the lowest and highest of these counts. Except in a very few casinos, the dealer can't stand on a "soft 17" (with an Ace that counts as 11) and must continue playing by hitting his hand. A count of 21 in two cards always beats 21 made with three or more cards unless the player gets 21 in a hand derived from splitting a pair of Aces or 10-value cards. Such a 21, if in two cards, is not a "natural" and counts as an ordinary 21 equal to the dealer's 21 made with three or more cards. A player winning on this type of 21 is paid even money on his bet and does not receive the Black Jack bonus.

All players play their individual hands against the dealer's. Blackjack tables have six or seven "holes" on the layout for the placing of bets, with accompanying chairs or stools for the players, arranged in a semicircle and all facing the dealer.

The dealer first deals a card to the player on his extreme left, then one to each additional player or to each hand being played, from left to right, and finally one to himself, and repeats this process until all players, or all hands if some players are betting on more than one, and the dealer each have two cards.

There are many variations in the layouts, in the amount of cards being used, the way they are dealt out and handled after the play is finished, and the house rules governing permissible action by players and the dealer, with the result that you may not find any two casinos that you visit conducting Blackjack in exactly the same manner.

One, two, or four decks may be used. When one or two decks are used the cards are usually held in the dealer's hand as they are being dealt out. An open-faced box, or *shoe*, is used in holding four decks. It remains on the table and the cards are withdrawn from it one at a time by the dealer.

Some casinos use all 52 cards in a single deck. The practice in others is to "burn" the top card, after the deck has been shuffled and cut, by taking it out of play and putting it face up at the bottom of the deck. If the top card is burned the last card in the deck isn't used either and the playing action is confined to the 50 cards in between. In using a full deck without burning a card, a Joker may be inserted at the place where the deck is cut and it marks the point at which the deck, or that portion of it not then in play, has to be reshuffled. Any player receiving the Joker will use it to cut the reshuffled deck, then the play is resumed with that player getting the first card in the new deal. If the dealer gets the Joker, the player to the dealer's extreme left does the cutting, then the play resumes with the dealer getting the first card to replace the Joker that marked the end of the previous deal.

The customary practice of the dealer picking up the used cards and placing them in his hand face up at the bottom of the deck below the burned card or the Joker has been the subject of unfavorable criticism. It could give opportunities for a dishonest dealer to cheat either the players or his employer. A dealer can easily pick up the discards in such a way that he has arranged to deal himself a good hand on the next play, or to hit his hand with a high card if he needs one, or to deal such a card to a player if that card might bust the player's hand. The dealer could also purposely bust his own hand if a player at the table is in collusion with him to do the casino out of some of its money. An alert player is likely to notice that one or more of the cards in the current play are the same ones that were used in the previous play, but who is going to complain about it when the dealer and a lone player are both partners in larceny?

A significant improvement recently started in some Nevada casinos is for the used cards to be stacked face down on a designated place on the layout. They won't be touched again until the dealer has to pick them up to shuffle them and have a player cut the deck. Then the dealer continues dealing from where the play was interrupted by exhaustion of the cards in his hand or in the shoe. Leaving the discards on the layout does away with the need for either a Joker or a burned card. A Joker, if present, is not involved in the playing and is merely a mechanical device to assist in cutting the deck. In a two- or four-deck game with the cards being drawn from the shoe, the used cards can be placed in back of the movable partition in the shoe, or stacked face down elsewhere, depending on how the house prefers this detail to be handled.

Descriptions that an Ace is never burned, and that if the top card happens to be an Ace the deck will be reshuffled and cut in an attempt to burn a card of another denomination, are not accurate as they apply to Nevada gambling. The dealer in Nevada doesn't even look at the burned card. From the way it is usually rolled to the bottom of the deck under cover of the dealer's palm it is evident that the house isn't too anxious for players to see it either.

If you want to know you can always ask. It's optional with the dealer to reveal it and he'll probably do so on your request. If you're mentally casing the full deck or just counting down Aces it's important for you to know what the burned card is. Any time a dealer refuses to disclose the burned card when you ask to see it, call for the pit boss and complain about the dealer's refusal. If the pit boss doesn't overrule the dealer and settle this complaint to your satisfaction, get up and quit playing Blackjack at that casino.

Elimination of inactive cards in the deal speeds up the game, and some casinos that used to burn the top card in a single deck now use all 52 of the cards. This also helps in eliminating any possible arguments about the burned card or just plain unexpressed discontent by players who may not be satisfied with the operation of burning the top card and not using the last one. While the house is primarily concerned with faster action and the avoidance of complaints, a casino in using all 52 cards in a single deck gives a definitely favorable break to the player who is able to take advantage of it. The cards can be more accurately counted down. When the used cards are stacked separately and not kept together with those that still have to be dealt, you can compare the two groups at a glance and form a reasonably accurate guess as to the proportion of each and how far the deal has progressed.

There are differences in the way the cards are dealt. With a single deck the first two cards given to players are delivered face down. They're usually all dealt face up when two or four decks are used. This is one of the reasons why experienced players prefer the game with multiple decks. In a single-deck game some of the other players may be extraordinarily secretive about their hands, and with the dealer snatching the cards the moment they're turned face up at the end of a play, this works against the player who needs to know what they are. The expert traditionally, but not always, plays at the hole farthest to the dealer's right, or the "third base" location, not only to play his hand after he has seen other players play theirs, but to better observe the identity of all the cards used. It's harder to do this when you're seated somewhere in the middle and trying to look in two different directions.

The dealer's first two cards are dealt to himself, one face up and one face down. There is no real difference to the average player which comes first, but there is a big difference to the casino and a good reason for it. The dealer's first card will be his face-up, or *showing*, card. The card the dealer receives face down is his *hole card*. When the hole card is the last one received, the dealer slides it under the showing card as part of his dealing motion. This is done to keep the back of the hole card covered, to make it almost impossible for a dishonest player to "read" it through any marks he may have placed on the back or on the edge of the card earlier during the course of his playing.

You have a big edge over the house if you know for sure that the dealer's hole card is, or isn't, an Ace or a 10-value card. One player was able to do that bit of mental deduction legitimately through the simple process of reversing the Aces and 10-value cards in his hand as he received them, and after a few deals he had all the high cards upside down. His success over the casino was nothing short of phenomenal and it excited the house's curiosity to learn why this player was consistently winning. It didn't take the house long to find out. The casino had been using "one-way" cards with back designs that were not symmetrical and this player was smart enough to take advantage of it. You can be sure that this error on the part of any gambling casino is not likely to be repeated, and you'll find that all cards used today have back designs that are exactly alike no matter how the cards are held.

After the first two cards to each hand, including the dealer's, are dealt all around, if the dealer's showing card is an Ace or a 10-value card he'll peek at his hole card without revealing it to players. If the dealer has a Black Jack he'll immediately announce it by turning up his hole card and he'll collect all bets except those by players who have Black Jack and stand off with him. It's also a stand-off for players who have fully insured their bets if the dealer's showing card was an Ace.

If the dealer doesn't have Black Jack, the play continues with the hand at the dealer's extreme left. The player looks at his two cards. If he thinks he has a good chance to beat the dealer's probable count he'll *stand*—play his hand as it is without any additional cards—and signify his intention by placing his cards, still face down if they were dealt to him that way, under his bet. If the player wants more cards he'll verbally ask for a "hit" or motion for one by waving his cards facing toward him, in front of him, or over his bet, with the emphasis on the movement away from the dealer and toward himself. He is dealt his third and any subsequent cards face up. If he stands on his three cards, he'll put the cards under his bet and perhaps also say "I stand," "I'm good," "That's enough," or any other words to the same effect. If he wants another hit he'll ask for it or motion for it. If his count goes over 21 he's *bust* and turns up his face-down cards, and the dealer picks up all that player's cards together with the player's losing bet.

This procedure is repeated with each hand being played, in its proper turn from the dealer's left to right, until the dealer plays his hand last.

In casinos outside Nevada where gambling has not attained the same high reputation for honesty on the part of employees, special rules may be in effect to prevent dealers from signaling the identity of the hole card to players who may be in collusion with them to cheat the casino. The dealer is not allowed to look at his hole card at any time before actually playing out his hand. If the dealer should get a Black Jack all bets are settled on the basis of the original bets by players, and no splits or doubled-down bets are recognized.

When the player goes bust he irrevocably loses and it makes no difference whether the dealer also goes bust later. The player's playing his hand first before the dealer acts on his own hand results in a hidden advantage to the house.

The Black Jack, or combination of two cards with a count of 21, when made with the first two cards dealt to a hand, has priority of action. If the player has it he immediately turns up his cards if they were dealt to him face down and he gets paid one and one-half times his bet. This payoff for the Black Jack is made even before the routine continuation of play that begins with the hand at the dealer's extreme left. The players who have anything else and who decide to stand on what their count is with two or more cards will have to wait until the dealer finally plays his own hand to learn whether the decision is a win, loss, or stand-off for them.

A player can elect to stand or hit at any time on any count he has, but the dealer is bound by certain rules which he can't change. The dealer has to play a single hand "straight," without any of the splitting or doubling-down options that are available to players under certain conditions.

The dealer must hit all counts of his hand up to and including 16, and usually also on "soft 17," which if made with two cards would be an Ace and a 6. At one time many years ago when the dealer had an Ace and a 6 it was considered a soft 17 if the dealer showed the Ace and he had to hit to it, and if he showed the 6 he had a "hard 17" and had to stand on it. That distinction no longer applies. The dealer stands on "hard 17," which has no Ace in it or has any Ace that is counted as 1. The dealer stands on all counts of 18, 19, 20, or 21.

Many of the dealers in Nevada casinos are unable to give you an accurate explanation of what a "soft 17" is when you ask them about it. This is not surprising, because if the dealers had been reading any gambling literature at all they easily could have picked up the wrong material and never corrected their original erroneous impressions. You might be told by a dealer that a soft 17 is a count of 17 with an Ace in it. That's not the right answer. A count of 9, 3, 4, and Ace, or Ace, 5, Ace and 10, adding up to 17, is *not* a soft 17.

An Ace in the dealer's hand *always* counts as 11 unless it brings the dealer's hand to over 21, in which case it is counted or revalued as 1 and the dealer then has to stand on his new hard count if it is 17, or hit on anything lower.

This explains why a dealer with an Ace and a 7 has to stand on 18 even though a lone player may have 19, 20, or 21. You would expect the dealer to give himself another hit in a desperate attempt to equal or beat the player's count, but that isn't allowed. This is one example of house rules that actually favor the players. A player having an Ace and a 7 can value his count as either 8 or 18 and can take a hit on it with safety. The player can't go bust on one hit on any soft count (with an Ace valued as 11), because the player can revalue his Ace as 1 if he has to.

In a few casinos the dealer has the option of either hitting or standing on a soft 17. In a single-deck game, where the players receive their first two cards face down, the dealer won't know what they are, unless a player goes bust, until he finishes playing his own hand. In multiple-deck games, where all cards to players are dealt face up, the dealer has some choice of action. When only one player is playing a single hand against the dealer, the dealer will stand on his soft 17 if he sees the player is standing on anything less. If the player shows a superior hand, the dealer, who has nothing to lose and everything to gain by it, is going to hit. What the dealer will do when there's a stand-off on 17 is anybody's guess. Maybe he follows instructions from his superiors, or maybe he is allowed to use his independent judgment.

Where more than one hand or more than one player are involved it is assumed that the dealer, being an employee of the house, is going to look after its best interests. The dealer may even stand on a soft 17 and accept a loss against three or four players having small bets, for example the $1 minimum, to get at another player who stands on a low count and will lose $5 or more as a result. Therefore, you can take it for granted that anytime the dealer can stand on a soft 17 with any advantage to the house, he will do so.

There are two very important betting options available to players. These are splitting pairs and "doubling down for one," which are described in detail a little further on in this chapter. I stress their importance because they're your real key to successful Blackjack playing if you're not an expert at it and do it the easy way. Another option, available in some casinos, is the *Insurance bet*. It isn't important to the average player. The expert who counts down the full deck and knows the number of 10-value cards in the remainder yet to be dealt, to which must be added the dealer's hole card, can turn betting on Insurance to his advantage. It will help increase his gains or cut down his losses, depending on how his general over-all luck is running.

You won't learn much by watching the average amateur gamblers play Blackjack. They're short on both the cash and the necessary know-how that have to be combined for the most effective playing. Few of the amateurs really know what they're doing or why they're doing it.

You'll learn something from the more experienced players, if not in a positive sense, at least in finding out what it is that they have and you don't have. Because Blackjack to some extent does test your skill and ability to do fast, accurate thinking, many players, while admittedly not experts, find the game extremely stimulating.

The expert Blackjack player commands attention. You will enjoy watching him in action for the same reason that you get pleasure from personal observation of any human activity that is performed with *finesse*. He may be playing only one hand, or he may be occupying all the holes at the table. If others are playing with him he may have chosen his companions himself to fully occupy all the holes at that table and keep strangers off it.

You may have been told by a dealer or a pit boss that you as an individual can't have more than three original hands in the same play, if there are available holes for them, so your obvious question is how someone else is playing six or seven of them. House rules governing how many holes a player can occupy are not rigid. They are flexible matters that can be the subject of direct verbal negotiation between the player and the casino. If you ask to do it and are allowed to play more than three hands, there may be conditions attached to the resulting informal verbal agreement.

You'll have to agree to bet a certain minimum amount on each hand if playing all the holes at the table, or at least the aggregate total of all those bets if you're playing a lesser number of hands. Let's say that the house allows you to play six hands on a layout having that many holes if your minimum bet on each hand is $5. If there's a play where you're only betting on two hands, your bets on those will have to be stepped up to a $15 minimum to keep up your part of the agreement. That minimum on single bets or on the total betting in a play could be much larger if you're competing with other well-financed players for the few available holes in a busy casino. It is recognized that at peak periods of business no casino is going to allow one player to monopolize a whole table unless the inducements, in terms of the size of his betting, are quite substantial.

The rules are relaxed for known big-money gamblers. Owners and managers of gambling casinos, prohibited by law from gambling in their own establishments, will frequently visit their rivals, where they are extended the full V.I.P. treatment, including the privilege of playing as many hands as they like and exclusive occupancy of the table.

The rule governing the average player and restricting him to no more than three hands can be easily circumvented. Bring a friend or two of yours to play alongside you. If you're furnishing all the cash for the gambling and your friends are technically nothing more than your own shills who will follow your instructions, then you have effectively cornered that table for yourself.

The expert big-money player will usually be playing alone. He has to, because it's essential for him to concentrate on what he's doing without any disturbing influences. His photographic memory for remembering which cards have been drawn from the deck, and which still remain undistributed, enables him to play more successfully than the inexperienced gambler who steps into the game blind. Toward the end of the deal when there are only a few cards left in the deck, accurate knowledge of what they are can often result in situations that can be manipulated to his advantage. The expert plays a waiting game, not betting or betting at or close to the minimum until he diagnoses something coming up that is to his liking; then he plunges heavily for as much as the house rules or his own finances will permit.

When to hit and when to stand, and when to double down or split pairs and when not to do it—educated guesses at best to most players—are an exact science with the expert. There are many possible situations that give the player a better than 50 percent chance of success. Sometimes the number of hands being played can be changed to the player's advantage.

If the four cards remaining in the deal at the beginning of a play are all 10-value cards and the player is playing one hand, the prognosis is a stand-off, with both player and dealer having 20. If the player can play four hands, either by direct permission of the house or through the trick of having a friend join in for some of the action, he'll take all those high cards and the dealer will have to depend on his luck for what he gets from a reshuffled deck to get a showing card that is as good or better than 10. Each of the four hands by the players, with a 10-value card as the first card received in each hand, gives the players individually and all together a decided temporary advantage over the dealer.

Where the five cards at the start of a play are two 6s and three 10s, the player who has been playing more than one hand can profitably cut down to one. Of the ten possible arrangements of the player's first two cards (in each case of course the other cards go to the dealer), the player will win with seven of them.

With a 5, 6, and three 10s, the margin in favor of the player is finer but still there if he knows how to play his hand, and capable strategy has its rewards. Ordinarily you would ask for a hit on your count of 15 against a dealer's 10 showing card, but here knowledge that the dealer will lose two of the three possible arrangements of 10, 10, and 6 justifies a stand on 15. The player getting two 10s will lose to the dealer's 21 in three cards if the 10s aren't split. Even at that the ten possible arrangements of the player's two or three cards against the remainder going to the dealer would result in five wins and five losses. The player will double down on 11 if he has the two low cards in his hand first and will finish with 21 against the dealer's 20 on that doubled bet, thus changing what might have been an even break to odds of 6 to 5 in his favor. The player's 20 in two cards would be a loser to the dealer's 21 in three, but that favorable prospect for the dealer can be thwarted by the player splitting his 10s, even against the dealer's showing 10, to bust it up. The player standing on 15 or 16 on one hand and on whatever he gets in a new deal for the second card in the other hand derived from the split would leave the dealer in a most unfavorable position. The dealer would have to hit to a count of 15 or 16 in his own hand, not with a certainty of beating the player, but with expectations about 3 to 2 that the dealer will be the loser, and with the house's liability increased on account of the split pair and the two bets riding on them.

I could go on for many pages with other situations that an expert would instantly recognize as the time for greatly increased betting. These few examples are sufficient to establish what I'm trying to demonstrate here—that a real expert can, even by sometimes playing contrary to the usual playing advice if he knows what he's doing, do better for himself than the average player.

The Black Jack bonus of 50 percent of the player's bet is involved in the strategy of all intelligent players, whether experts or just ordinarily good ones. Figured from a full deck of 52 cards, four of them, or one out of thirteen, will be Aces, but if your actual count-down of Aces in a deck partially used shows a proportion of them greater than $\frac{1}{13}$ of the cards remaining to be dealt, there is a better than normal probability of your obtaining a Black Jack. The 10-value cards must be considered too, but since there are sixteen of them compared to four Aces the probability of using them all up before the four Aces is relatively remote. Most players who do not case the deck completely are satisfied just to count the Aces. Having 50 or 100 percent more Aces than normal—for example, three where there should be two, or two where there should be one—will take care of all but the most extremely unfavorable fluctuations in the number of 10-value cards remaining that can couple with an Ace to form your Black Jack.

The smart player bets more heavily when the probability

of obtaining an Ace is better than $\frac{1}{13}$, and drops out or only bets small amounts at other times unless certain other factors justify increased bets. You can innocently come into these favorable situations even without counting down Aces if you stagger the amount of your bets, starting low and regularly increasing them toward the end of the deal. This can best be done when playing alone against the dealer. Instead of making $10 bets all the time, if that's your average, start with $6 and increase your bet by $1 on each play until it reaches the $14 or $15 maximum at the end of the deal. When the Aces are concentrated toward the end of the deal and you get your Black Jack then when the probability for it is greatest and you have more of your money on your bet, it will work to your profit. Your playing takes on added interest because you're not only gambling on getting a Black Jack but also on when it comes in the deal. Needless to say, this strategic maneuver is not available to the players who never bet more than the table minimum at any time.

If all the Aces or most of them are used up early in the deal, and you don't even have to be counting them to notice that, you can cut down on your bets or drop out for the remainder of the deal. If you're playing alone and don't desire to continue betting during that deal, you can ask the dealer to reshuffle the cards and start all over. This is an unusual request for a player to make, but I can see no possible reason that any casino can give for not complying with it. Of course, if other players are at the same table you might have to obtain their consent, and if they had any objections your request for an immediate reshuffle might not be granted even though the house otherwise would be very happy to have the dealer reshuffle the deck at any time.

One or more Aces and some 10-value cards in the last part of the deal, when less than thirteen cards remain, present some fascinating possibilities for the player who is intent on exploiting the advantage of the Black Jack bonus.

Suppose that the four remaining cards are an Ace and three 10-value cards. The offhand uneducated guess is that either the dealer or the player who gets the Ace will be the winner, and it's a 50—50 gamble that it can fall either way.

There's more to it than that. If the player gets the Black Jack, a probability of two out of the four possible arrangements of the mentioned cards, the house will pay him one and one-half times his bet. The dealer can also get the Black Jack two out of four times. When the dealer does it after showing his 10-value card, it's the dealer's win, pure and simple, over the player. But if the dealer shows his Ace, the player can bet on Insurance if he's playing in a casino where this type of bet is handled, and instead of losing, the player will stand off thanks to the Insurance, which was 100 percent in his favor. So you would have, considering everything, two chances of your winning 150 percent of your bet against one chance of losing the bet and one chance of a stand-off if the bet is fully insured.

When one or more Aces are in the few remaining cards in the deal, it is important for the player to get them—first to enjoy the Black Jack probability, which may be several times greater than normal, and second to keep an Ace out of the dealer's hand if that is possible. Let's say that the deal at the start of a play is down to the last three cards, all Aces. A player regularly betting one hand against the dealer, knowing that, will expand to three hands and will get all of those Aces. Then from the reshuffled 49 other cards in the deck, assuming there are no other players, he has almost a one-third chance, 16 out of 49, of coupling a 10-value card to any of his Aces to get a Black Jack. The Black Jack probability, 1 chance in $20\frac{23}{32}$ in a full deck, has been boosted up to 1 chance in $3\frac{1}{16}$, and the player has three different hands with that probability, not just one. If the dealer's showing card has a value other than 10, the player's Black Jack probability improves to exactly 1 out of 3, and with three tries at it he'll average one Black Jack with normal luck. At the same time the probability of the dealer's getting a Black Jack in the same play to stand off with the player has been reduced to far below the expectancy of 9 times out of 245 when considered with a full deck.

Players who count down Aces should bet heavily when the climate for Black Jack is much improved—not just double, but maybe 10, 50, or 100 times the amount of their regular betting at other times, to make the most of this advantage.

In addition to the Black Jack bonus of 50 percent of the bet, which is the same in all casinos, a very few of the casinos offer bonus payments for certain combinations of cards other than the Black Jack. These extra bonus payments don't interest the expert players much because they come so infrequently or pay off so little that they don't affect the expert's gambling strategy. They do, nevertheless, provide an attraction for the average player. *Other things being equal,* your playing in a casino that offers such extra bonus payments is better than playing in another casino that doesn't offer them. The casino making these bonus payments can justifiably point to itself as being more generous than its competitors.

A player's hand of 21, made with three 7s, on which some of the extra bonus payments may be made, can come once in 5525 players' hands if the hand is played to include three cards. The formula is $\frac{4}{52} \times \frac{3}{51} \times \frac{2}{50}$ when figured from a full deck. If you have a pair of 7s you may decide that it's more to your advantage to split them than to ask for a hit on a count of 14. A 6, 7, and 8 of the same suit, carrying the probability formula $\frac{12}{52} \times \frac{2}{51} \times \frac{1}{50}$, also gives you 1 chance in 5525 if you stretch your hand to three cards. You might have two of the cards and would prefer to stand on them if the dealer shows a low card. Operators of casinos that offer these bonuses frankly admit that they're designed to encourage players with counts of 13, 14, or 15 to hit to their hands, with some probability that they'll go bust. Diverting them from splitting a pair of

7s when they should do it also works to the house's advantage.

A bonus payment is sometimes made on a player's count of 21 with seven cards in it. An Ace somewhere along the line would almost certainly bring your hand to a decision before you accumulated as many as six cards and still felt the need for another one. The lowest count that you could have in six cards without an Ace would be 2, 2, 2, 2, 3, and 3, adding up to 14.

If an extra bonus is paid on the Ace and Jack of Spades, it represents a pure gift by the house because there is no possible advantage the house could get by offering it, and it doesn't affect the strategy of the players. The player can expect to get this combination once in 1326 hands.

These bonus payments are only for players' original hands. The bonus payment, usually $5, is payable to any player having a bet for $1 or more, and if the bet is less than $1 the bonus is correspondingly reduced. A 50-cent bet would qualify a player for a $2.50 bonus, and a 25-cent bet for a $1.25 bonus.

On the 25-cent-minimum tables in downtown Reno or Las Vegas, the regular Black Jack payoff of one and one-half times the bet would amount to 37½ cents and can't be conveniently made, so the casino pays double and gives you 50 cents for a Black Jack. This increased Black Jack bonus to make the payoff double the size of your bet is for the minimum 25-cent bet only.

In 10,000 hands a player could expect to have about seven Black Jacks with the Ace and Jack of Spades, one hand of 21 with three 7s when the dealer showed a high card and the player chose to hit to his 14 rather than stand on it or split the pair of 7s, and one hand with 6, 7, and 8 of the same suit also made against the dealer's high showing card. The nine extra bonus payments, amounting to $45, would represent a gift of 45 cents on each $100 of betting by the player who bets $1 on each hand. The attraction would diminish for a player whose average bet is larger than $1, and for the big-money gambler it would almost disappear altogether. Nevertheless, a $5 extra payment by the house, coming on top of your Black Jack bonus or your win on a count of 21, is not hard to take.

I should warn you not to fall into the trap of making the extra bonus payments the sole reason for your playing in any casino that offers them, or you'll find yourself in the same position as the housewife who is more interested in collecting trading stamps than in comparing prices and shopping where she can make her purchases at the lowest net cost.

I presume that the average reader of this book is one whose reputation for playing Blackjack would not strike fear into the hearts of casino owners or managers, and that being so, the house will welcome you and as much money as you can bring with you.

In your counting down Aces or in any more refined elaboration of casing the deck, it has to be done mentally. A counting case such as is used in Faro or a pocket-sized Oriental abacus would be ideal for this purpose but could not be employed at any Blackjack table. It is mandatory in some casinos, and the usual procedure in all of them, for the dealer to shuffle the cards at any time except in the middle of a play when the dealer becomes aware that the cards are being cased—for example, if he observes one of the players making written notes. Some casinos also make it a practice to shuffle the deck before any play on which the table maximum is being bet on a hand.

Can you withdraw a bet already made or change its amount? Yes, you can, under certain very limited conditions. If you made a big bet and then observed that the dealer was shuffling the cards after you put your money down, thus destroying any advantage you think you may have had by your casing the deck mentally or counting down Aces up to that point, you can withdraw from the action altogether or cut down the size of your bet, but you have to think and act fast. In the single-deck game, once you have been dealt a card, whether you have looked at it or not, your bet as it stands in the hole must remain unchanged except for any permitted additional betting by splitting pairs or doubling down, until a decision is reached on the play in progress. In the multiple-deck game, the first card dealt face up to any player freezes all the initial betting action at that table, including bets by players not yet reached by the dealing.

Minimum and maximum bets vary with the house rules, and besides being different from one casino to another, there may be tables with different limits in the same casino, or the limit on one table might change at different times during the day. Information about limits is supposed to be posted at the table or on a sign prominently displayed close to it, but I found that many casinos are delinquent in publicizing this necessary bit of information.

In some casinos when the minimum table limit is $1 on a single hand and you're betting that minimum, you can bet on an additional hand if there's an unoccupied hole by betting a minimum of $2 on that second bet. The second hand you play can immediately follow your first hand and does not have to be placed where the unoccupied hole is. This total minimum of $3 on the two bets can be split and, if you want to, you can put $1.50 on each bet. Betting on a third hand, under similar conditions, calls for a minimum of $5 on the third hand. The sum of $8 can be split any way you like as long as there's at least $1 on each bet and the total comes to $8 or more. If you're betting the same amount on each hand you would probably be making $3 bets.

In other casinos the $2 and $5 bets on the second and third hands, respectively, must also be matched by raising the other bets to those amounts. That is, you have to bet at least $2 on *each* hand when playing two of them, and at least $5 on *each* hand when betting on three hands. On $5-minimum tables there are no such requirements on additional hands except that your minimum bets, whether on one, two, or three hands, have to be for at least that advertised minimum.

My first studies of Blackjack were by imitation, following the "never go bust" theory of many of the players who won't take a hit on any hard count of 12 or higher. By studying its operation for some time I was able to pick up a few nuggets of information useful to a player who insists on playing this way in spite of all advice against it.

In repeated samples of playing, with a player standing on any stiff score, I observed that when the dealer had to hit his own count of 12 to 16 inclusive, the dealer invariably lost between 58 and 62 percent of the time if we ignored the few stand-offs. This percentage remained fairly constant whether the player's performance as a whole was good, bad, or indifferent. These situations did not include all hands in which the dealer had three or more cards, but they were numerous enough to justify the broad assumption that when the dealer's showing card was 2 to 6, the dealer would lose more often than he won if the player took no chances on going bust.

Therefore, I concluded, when the dealer's showing card is a low one, 2 to 6, the player should split *all* pairs and double down on his count of 9, 10, or 11 on all recommended occasions, and when the dealer shows a high card the player should split only Aces and 8s and never double down unless he has a count superior to the dealer's showing card, and one on which he could make more by doubling down than by playing a straight single hand. Further study was needed to define exceptions or marginal cases slightly in favor of or against the player, but the basic theory is still valid. It is a good one for players who play Blackjack the easy way.

In casinos that allow you to double down on any count on your first two cards or on any count at any time in two or more cards, you have increased opportunities for doubling down that can be followed. A bold player will capitalize on the dealer's bust probability, which is over 40 percent when the dealer shows a 4, 5, or 6 and will double down on any count less than 12 and on any soft hand, gambling that the dealer will go bust. Doing this should be compared to making hard-way bets in Craps—that is, do it only when you're ahead of the game and can afford to press your luck with money that you have already won from the house.

Doubling on any count of 12 or higher is usually against the average player and shouldn't be attempted. The expert can do it if he's accurately casing the deck and knows what to expect. If the last few cards are all relatively low ones, in the range from 5 to 7, the expert with a count of 14 who can double on that will do so and will have a much improved hand with the prospects of winning twice as much on it.

Recommendations for the player's hitting to his count when it is 12 or more are made by all gambling authorities. How good are they? I found that by following a simple plan of standing on any hard count over 11 if the dealer shows a low card, and hitting everything up to and including 16 if the dealer shows a high card, the player will do much better than by standing on all stiffs or hitting on all counts up to and including 16 regardless of what the dealer is showing. This easily remembered formula is subject to further variations and refinements by the various experts, and I would endorse any of them as basically sound advice. For example, it is slightly to the player's advantage to take a hit on 12 when the dealer shows 2 or 3.

Few casino managements care to comment on what they earn at Blackjack, but those that do place their earnings from play by average players at between 2 and 3 percent of their betting. This confirms my own observations, which were independently arrived at. The house will earn more from players who stand on all stiffs or who imitate the dealer and hit all hands under 17; it will earn less from those players who follow a "tough" basic strategy and supplement that with aggressively splitting pairs and doubling down whenever possible under favorable conditions. So, a precise figure for the house percentage in Blackjack could only be calculated if the game were restricted to a specified strategy by the player and a specified set of rules by the house governing the splitting of pairs and doubling down.

The basic house percentage given by Dr. Edward O. Thorp in his book, *Beat the Dealer,* if his playing recommendations are followed, is 0.21 percent, and that low figure can be still further reduced by liberal house rules regarding splitting of pairs and doubling down. I doubt if a basic strategy favoring the player exists, because of some of the house rules which limit splitting and doubling.

You will readily see here that a little more efficiency on the part of the player, counting down Aces and betting more heavily at times to take advantage of the Black Jack bonus, can swing the percentage advantage in the player's favor. House rules vary from one casino to another. You may get the impression, particularly right here, that house rules are always designed to frustrate the player or to increase the house's earnings on a certain game or type of bet. That is not necessarily so, and a lot of the rules currently in effect actually favor the players over the house if you know when and how to take advantage of them.

Blackjack rules throughout Las Vegas were drastically tightened in April 1964 as a result of players winning there by successfully putting Dr. Thorp's advice into practice. Thus, for the first time, rules for splitting pairs and doubling down were essentially the same in all Las Vegas casinos.

The new Las Vegas playing rules permitted you to double down only on a count of 11 made with the first two cards in your hand. Splitting a pair of Aces was no longer allowed.

The average, non-expert players who furnished the bulk of the casinos' patronage and income from Blackjack didn't play when they found the new "very tight" rules for splitting pairs and doubling down not to their liking. This meant a big drop in gross income from Blackjack for the Las Vegas casinos.

It was at first expected that casinos throughout Nevada would follow Las Vegas in adopting similar Blackjack rules, but this did not happen. Many of the big money gamblers who play nothing but Blackjack, who used to play regularly in Las Vegas, went to the northern Nevada casinos to play. Casinos in Reno and elsewhere welcomed the increased patronage and said they have no intention of losing business by imitating the new Las Vegas rules. The playing rules in the northern Nevada casinos remained unchanged.

Any further tightening of playing rules in Las Vegas, such as complete elimination of the doubling down option, reduction of the Black Jack bonus, or dealing the first two cards of the dealer's hand face down, could have killed the goose that lays the golden egg.

It is my feeling that Nevada casino managements should be thankful to Dr. Thorp for stimulating more public interest in the game of Blackjack. Blackjack has always earned money for the casinos, and if they should have to operate in the future on a smaller profit margin due to more efficient players, that lower percentage will be more than made up for by an increased volume of money in action.

It was difficult to evaluate the expressed alarm or the lamentations of Las Vegas casino owners, who sometimes moan and groan even in situations that could greatly benefit them financially.

In the competitive Nevada gambling picture no casino can afford to make too many rules that work against the players or it will get a reputation of being too tight, and discriminating gamblers will stay away from it in droves. It must be recognized that some rules are for the protection of the house, and these rules are substantially the same throughout the business.

The house has several defenses against a player who

has both the necessary intelligence and the capital required to put it at a probable disadvantage that could cost it a lot of money. The limits can be lowered, the dealer can be instructed to shuffle the cards when the deck is half used to prevent players from casing the last half of it, and in extreme cases the player can be barred from playing altogether.

Important to you as a Blackjack player is selecting a casino where you're allowed to take any of the 10-value cards, whether alike or dissimilar in rank, as a pair and split them into two hands. If the first card dealt to you is a 10-value card, you have a five times better chance (15 out of 51 when considered from a full deck) to complete a pair with any other 10-value card than to draw another card of the same rank where your chance is only 3 out of 51. On drawing a third 10-value card to the first hand in a split 10-value pair, your chances are 35 times better (210 in 2550) than getting a third card of the same rank where the probability drops to only 6 in 2550.

Both cards in a split pair are turned face up if you received them face down, and on splitting the pair into two hands you place your original bet on one of the hands and duplicate that bet on the other. The hand nearer the dealer's left in a split pair is played to completion before the second card is dealt to the second hand derived from the split and that hand is played out.

If you're restricted to having exact pairs such as two Queens in splitting 10-value cards, your chances of splitting all original hands are only about 45 percent of what they would be otherwise, and you can see that your chances of getting a third or a fourth card of the same denomination to split again decline very sharply.

In a single-deck game one pair of 10-value cards, if not restricted in any way, can be expanded to a possible maximum of 16 hands. In some of the Las Vegas casinos I was told that you could make the $500 maximum bet, stretch an original pair into 16 hands; then, after having all the

10-value cards, you could double down on a count of 12 with total safety, and on 13 also if you received all of the 9s first; with the result that you could have $10,000 or more of your money at stake on what started as a $500 bet, to be settled by the playing of the dealer's hand. It would be a tremendous windfall for the player if the dealer went bust.

The possibilities are even greater in playing with two or four decks, where there are either 32 or 64 of the 10-value cards, if a lot of them are bunched up right at the spot where it's your turn to draw cards from the deck to complete your hands. In actual practice you may never be making anywhere near the maximum possible number of splits, but there will be plenty of times when one pair of 10-value cards can be stretched into four, five, six, or more hands. I emphasize your need to have a large amount of ready cash in reserve to press these opportunities to the utmost, because without being able to bet, your chance to split is lost.

I don't know of any casino allowing a player to split dissimilar 10-value cards that does not let the player go as far as he can on it. It is possible that at some time in the future a limit might be placed to offer some protection to both the house and the players. If such a limit is ever put into effect it would probably be at four hands, which is the maximum number that you can get from splitting any other value in a single deck, with limits of eight and sixteen hands respectively in games with two or four decks.

In splitting a pair of Aces you are only allowed one hit to each Ace, which would be the same as in doubling down to a count of 11. You should always split Aces, no matter what the dealer is showing. There are several compelling reasons, both positive and negative, for this advice. Under ordinary conditions you have almost a one-third chance to draw a 10-value card to your Ace and have a count of 21. You know the dealer doesn't have Black Jack if you're allowed to split, so your 21 won't lose against anything the dealer is able to stand on. Your Ace, counting as 11, gives you a temporary numerical advantage over any showing card by the dealer that is lower. Finally, if you don't split you'll be stuck with a count of either 2 or 12, both relatively poor hands to hit to.

A pair of 6s adding up to 12 should be split for the same reason when opposed to the dealer's showing card of 2 to 7. When the dealer shows 8, 9, 10, or Ace, the split would be unwise because the dealer would still have a big initial advantage, and you might as well sweat out your bad luck with minimum possible loss. The same goes for splitting 2s and 3s—do it when the dealer's showing card is not higher than 7.

Splitting 5s is not recommended at any time by other authors. I do it myself in my easy way, playing against a dealer's low showing card, if the house allows you to double on a hand derived from a split pair. Your getting a 4 or 6 in addition to the 5 you already have gives you an occasion for doubling down, and if you draw another 5 you can either double down on 10 or resplit once more. The aim is to get as much money in action as you can. Playing conservatively you would count two 5s as 10 and double on that, if the situation calls for a doubled bet, and never split the 5s.

Splitting 7s follows the same pattern as with 6s, but with the splits recommended against the dealer's showing card of 2 to 8. Splitting 8s is always indicated against anything the dealer shows to give you a better chance of success than if you stand on 16 or ask for a hit to that count.

Most gambling authorities recommend splitting 9s except when the dealer shows a 7, where your standing on 18 gives you a good chance to win and a splitting up of the pair of 9s would weaken that opportunity.

Authorities also tell you never to split 10s. I agree with this advice which can be supported statistically, but there are some good reasons why a player might want to split under certain conditions. The increased opportunities for splitting any two 10-value cards, in casinos that allow it, have already been discussed.

You would unhesitatingly double down on your count of 10 in two or more cards against a dealer's showing card of 2 to 9, figuring you have some advantage in doing so, so what's wrong with taking that count in a single card and getting two separate tries at it by the split pair? Your performance in terms of percentage of these bets won should be better on these than by doubling down on the same value, because if you should draw a low card as the second card in a hand derived from the split, you can ask for one or more hits to try to improve your hand if the dealer shows a high card. In casinos that allow you to split any two 10-value cards and resplit without limit, I would prefer to split them to get as many playing hands as possible when the dealer has a low showing card.

Splitting a pair of 10s to break up a count of 20 always leaves the other players, and sometimes the dealer, stunned in open-mouthed amazement. The emotional response is less interesting to many serious players than the fact that they think it's more profitable to play Blackjack this way. While I can't endorse this radical departure from previously accepted playing strategy without reservations, no one can deny that it makes the game more interesting.

The other betting option vital to players is "doubling down for one." This means that the player agrees to accept only one more card to the hand he already has, on the condition that he will increase the amount of his original bet. It is subject to more variations than splitting pairs, where the only difference is whether or not you were restricted to exact pairs of the same denomination in splitting the 10-value cards.

The mechanical process of doubling is simple. If you're playing with a single deck you take the first two cards which you received face down and turn them up, and these, with or without any hits that you might have received face up according to permissible house rules, form the hand on which you're doubling. In a game with two or four decks, your cards are probably already face up. You then receive one more card, this one face down, and it is not revealed until after the dealer plays out his own hand.

Incidentally, you need not double your bet. Any increase over the original bet is allowed. You'll either win or lose the amount you have on the hole for that bet when a decision for or against you is reached. You can increase your bet *up to* an added amount equal to your original bet, which is the maximum possible increase, and the betting option gets its name from this.

This little-known feature of doubling down is worth being acquainted with. You may reach a time when you're temporarily short on cash—for example, when you have a $10 bet on the original hand and less than $10 in uncommitted cash or chips. If the situation calls for doubling down and you can't put $10 more on the bet, it's all right and advisable to add $5 or $6 or whatever amount you can spare if the prospects of a win on the doubled bet look good to you—for example, when you're doubling down on your count of 11 against a dealer's low showing card.

A partial increase for less than the amount of the original bet could also work to the satisfaction (but probable financial disadvantage) of the extremely cautious player. For example, if you're making a small increase when your count shows a numerical superiority of one over the dealer's showing card, a bigger increase when you're two points above the dealer, and the full doubled amount for a superiority of three points or better, you may reason that you'll risk less on the bets where your chance of success is relatively lower.

Personally, I would recommend your going for the full doubled amount every time you double down if you have the money to double your bet, or not doubling down at all for a partial increase except, as in the example just described, when you're temporarily short on cash. You weaken your probable final stand to a lesser or greater degree by limiting yourself to one added card in doubling down. If after this weakening process you still have a better than 50 percent chance of beating the dealer, you've already paid the price for taking this option and you'll gain most from it by making the full doubled bet, not anything less.

Depending on the casino where you're playing, the house rules will allow you to double down for one under one of the following conditions:

1. You can double down on any count at any time regardless of the number of cards in your hand.
2. You can double down on any count but only on your first two cards.
3. You can double down on any count of 9, 10, or 11 regardless of the number of cards in your hand.
4. You can double down on 9, 10, or 11 but only on your first two cards.
5. You can double down on 10 or 11 regardless of the number of cards in your hand.
6. You can double down on 10 or 11 but only on your first two cards.
7. You can double down on 11 but only on your first two cards.

In addition, some casinos won't allow you to double down with any hand that includes an Ace, and some may not allow you to double down on a hand derived from a split. It is important, therefore, that you ask the dealer exactly what you can double down on before you start playing. If the dealer doesn't give you an explanation that is intelligible to you, repeat your questions directly to the pit boss. The pit bosses in many instances will try to brush you off with the excuse that they're "too busy," but any time the dealer can't and the pit boss won't answer questions about the casino games, take your business elsewhere. It wouldn't hurt to write to the management to explain why. If more efficiency or courtesy on the part of the employees is needed by the gambling public, maybe you'll eventually get it if you take your legitimate complaints directly to the top management level of the casinos.

In one northern Nevada casino I noticed that the customary sign explaining the house rules for splitting pairs and doubling down was not being exhibited at the Blackjack tables. I asked one of the dealers what those rules were, and the answer I got was: "I don't know—the boss will have to explain that to you—and I'm sure he won't." The dealer was right. The pit boss gave me no information whatever.

My personal experience, both in actual Nevada playing and in extended statistical projects under playing conditions that exactly duplicate the play at the casinos, is that I will win close to two thirds of all doubled bets on decisions other than stand-offs. Therefore, doubling down should be done as often as expediency and the house rules allow it. A player, at a casino with a fairly "tight" doubling-down policy, who takes full advantage of his limited opportunities, could do better than another player in a more liberal casino who is not aware of what he can do or is not doing it. It's not enough sometimes just to have the breaks in your favor. You have to recognize them and make them work for you.

Your net gains by doubling down are an essential part of the strategy of chopping away at the house percentage that is built into the game. Without extensively splitting pairs and doubling down, the average player is automatically licked.

If you play at a casino where you can double down on anything and your hand includes an Ace, the dealer will probably remind you that you have 19 or 20 or whatever your count is if it's a soft one, and that you might have a winning hand if you stand on your full count with your Ace valued at 11, instead of doubling on a count 10 points lower. If you insist on evaluating a 9 and an Ace as 10 and doubling on it you certainly can, but the dealer wants to

be sure that you know what you're doing. If you were un-
lucky and swapped what would have been one win for two
losses, you won't hold the casino responsible for your mis-
fortune.

There is a profit to the player over the house in doubling
down in the following situations when the player accepts
one more card to the count he already has, but not all of
them can be recommended as the best bets for the player
to make. In some of the marginal instances where a doubled bet is profitable you can make even more by playing
your hand straight without doubling, to stand when your
final count reaches or exceeds a planned minimum level.

Doubling down on your count of 10 or 11 against the
dealer's showing Ace, while not actually showing an over-
all profit, is also included because the reduction of your
net loss makes it a desirable action to take. You would lose
more if you didn't double down.

When you have a count of	You'll show a net gain over the house or reduce your possible loss when you double down against the dealer's showing card of
11	anything
10	anything but a 10 or picture card
9	7 or less
8	6 or 5

In addition to these, which mathematically favor the
player over the house on the average, there are numerous
other instances that will tempt the more adventurous gambler who doesn't mind bucking a percentage against him if
that percentage isn't too high. The expert who is accurately
casing the deck goes by the actual situation, not by published guides. If he sees that only low cards remain in the
deal, he could prefer to play his hand straight and draw as

many cards as he wants rather than double down to get stuck with a low final count.

Blackjack is not a game for timid souls. Like a Poker player trying to complete an inside straight, the gambler who is daring and lucky can make his playing strategy pay off.

The Insurance bet, where it is offered, means that the house is willing to lay 2 to 1 when the dealer is showing an Ace that the dealer won't have a Black Jack. Your bet, from the player's point of view, is that the dealer *will* get a Black Jack.

The Insurance bet is settled separately from any of the other betting. It may be made for any amount up to half what the player has on his original hand or hands. If made for that amount, your 2 to 1 win on it balances your loss on your regular betting, assuming that you didn't get a Black Jack. Because it's a stand-off, the win on Insurance against the loss of the regular betting, the dealer leaves all those bets undisturbed on the table and you're free to pick them up.

When the dealer's showing card is an Ace, there will be a pause in the dealing either after the showing card or after both of the dealer's cards have been dealt. The dealer will ask if anyone wants to bet on Insurance. When all the players and the dealer have two cards each, the dealer will then peek at his hole card and turn it up if he has Black Jack, and he'll pay players 2 to 1 on anything they have bet on Insurance.

This bet can't be made for more than half the player's regular betting and is restricted to those players who take Insurance on their own bets. That is, a player or an observer can't be making the Insurance bet on another's hand if that other player did not happen to take Insurance on it. If this were permitted it would be possible for anyone to bet on Insurance only under such favorable conditions that it would guarantee a profit and take the gamble out of gambling. The house allows the Insurance bet only because, in losing it, it hopes to collect the player's regular bet on which the Insurance was based. When both player and dealer have Black Jack the Insurance bet is still good if made; then the player has a profit of twice his Insurance bet instead of a stand-off with the dealer.

Ordinarily there is a slight advantage to the house. If the dealer shows an Ace, the chance of a Black Jack being completed with one of the other cards in the deck, including the dealer's hole card, which is the crucial one, is 16 out of 51 when figured from a full deck.

The practical, expert gambler is interested in actualities, not theoretical calculations based on the composition of a full deck, and will make the Insurance bet only when he's counting down the deal and the 10-value cards left in it and sees that there is a probability of one third or better that the dealer will get a Black Jack. When made under these conditions and not at any other time, the expert gambler will win between 40 and 50 percent of the Insurance bets he makes. The 2 to 1 payoff makes it an attractive proposition when you can break even financially on a 33⅓ percent win record and anything better shows a profit. That profit, to be sure, is not very large compared to the total regular betting, but every little bit helps, even if it only amounts to a small fraction of 1 percent.

A player is allowed to look at his cards before deciding to bet on Insurance. To a player, the most frustrating time for the dealer to have Black Jack is when the player has 20. I've seen players make the Insurance bet only at that time, an indication that they were motivated more by emotion than logic. Your having two 10s in your hand decreases the probability that the dealer will have a Black Jack. I would bet on Insurance only as the experts do, when I can expect a probability of success that is 33⅓ percent or better.

In concluding this chapter I'll sum up my Blackjack advice to the average player in an easy-to-read, easy-to-remember table. I invite your testing it against any other published Blackjack advice. No two experts agree on all the details about how the game should be played. Testing one basic strategy, or comparing it with another when done at home under exact Nevada casino operating conditions, makes an interesting form of solitaire or indoor family entertainment that can be very informative.

You should be able to get any casino's house rules in

Playing Blackjack the Easy Way

Standing or Hitting

When dealer shows	*hit to*	*stand on*
2, 3, 4, 5, or 6	11 or lower soft 17 or lower	12 or higher soft 18 or higher
7, 8, or 9	16 or lower soft 18 or lower	17 or higher soft 19 or higher
10-value card or Ace	15 or lower soft 18 or lower	16 or higher soft 19 or higher

Splitting Pairs

When dealer shows	*split*
2, 3, 4, 5, or 6	all pairs*
7	2s, 3s, 6s, 7s, 8s, Aces
8	7s, 8s, Aces
9, 10-value card, or Ace	8s and Aces

Doubling Down for One

When your count is	*double down if dealer shows*
11	anything
10	anything but a 10-value card
9	2, 3, 4, 5, or 6

* This is bold playing strategy. The conservative player will never split 5s or 10s and will split 4s only when the dealer shows a 5.

full detail for Blackjack, as it is conducted in that casino, by writing to it.

Author's recommendation about Blackjack: It all depends on your skill in playing and in managing your bets, and your luck.

CHAPTER 11

GETTING MORE ACTION FOR YOUR MONEY

Employees at gambling casinos will tell you that no system is any good. They feel they should know better than others. They're right on the spot, eight hours daily, watching customers go broke with monotonous regularity. It doesn't seem to make much difference what system, if any, is being used.

That is perfectly true if any gambling project is carried to infinity. However, the gambling activity of any one human being, even if he spends his entire lifetime at it, falls far short of infinity. It's not so much the imperfections of a system or the lack of one but a shortage of sufficient starting and operating capital that brings about the rapid downfall of the average amateur gambler. If you make sucker bets, risk too much at one time, or fail to take advantage of favorable sequences in the decisions of the dice by neglecting to cover every opportunity that is presented, you can exhaust your already insufficient capital very rapidly.

One of the motivating purposes in my research was to study how and why gamblers go broke and to devise a program of management to reduce that probability as much as possible.

In studies covering more than one million consecutive rolls in Craps, it was found that to be reasonably (but not completely) safe from going broke you need a capitalization of at least 1000 times your initial betting unit.

The probability of your getting that far behind if you follow a conservative plan of management is very remote. The gambling casinos themselves give you very sound advice when they tell you to risk no more than you can afford to lose and to divide that into small amounts to better withstand a siege of bad luck—which no gambler can avoid indefinitely.

Some of the gambling advice you get from self-styled experts is positively dangerous to all but persons so rich that they don't need to gamble. Some gambling advisers propose that you should start off big, let your money ride (if you're winning) until it reaches the table limit, then, if luck is with you a little while longer, with big bets, you'll win big. An advocate of this theory lays his claim to expertness in this field because he once helped a gambler who was down to his last $40 and, by following this plan, the gambler soon built that $40 into several thousand dollars. If it worked for him, it should work for you. At least, that's what you're led to believe.

Let's go into some basic mathematics here. Starting with a $10 bet, seven successive wins on line bets, with the bets progressively doubled, will boost that $10 up to $640. The table limit in most casinos is $500. Getting seven successive passes (or winning seven line bets in a row, no matter which way the dice go as long as your guesses are correct) is a probability of 1 chance out of 141. One loss anywhere short of the final objective will cancel all your gains and leave you with a $10 deficit. Forty dollars risked in this manner will give you four tries on a real long-shot proposition. Just four losing bets, and they don't have to be consecutive, will leave you broke. If he had put the whole $40 on the line as his initial betting unit, he would only have to win five bets in a row to reach the table limit, a probability of 1 in slightly over 34. Admittedly he was lucky, but that's not how I would advise anyone with $40 to do his gambling. You could, with just about equal disregard for the risk of losing, shoot the works on a single-throw bet on any hard-way number in Craps, or put it all on a straight play on the Roulette layout.

When you're playing as a shill, if your betting isn't re-

stricted by the house rules, or if you're playing with someone else's money, you can throw caution to the winds because you won't lose anything personally. If you lose such
a long-shot attempt, which is what you should expect almost all of the time, you can shrug your shoulders, turn to
the fellow whose money you were using and say, "Sorry,
pal, we lost!" Gamblers with very limited resources, playing with their own money, tend to be conservative with it
and that's the way I think it ought to be. You may be
called a coward for not risking much of your capital at
one time, but don't let such stabs at your pride upset you.

I have on numerous occasions in my research built up a
$40 start into a five- or six-figure nest egg without incurring
the risks that are inherent in any do-or-die gambling plan.
Later chapters in this book will tell you how you can do it.

If the amount you can afford to lose is $100 or less, the
best thing you can do for yourself is to go to a gambling
casino where you can play Craps with 10-cent betting units.
You can find these casinos in the downtown areas of both
Reno and Las Vegas. If you have to begin playing at a
higher minimum, adjustments should be made in the
amounts of your succeeding bets if you start off winning,
so that your larger bets are related to the 10-cent betting
unit. Otherwise, the maximum losses you might suffer will
be more than you can afford with your very limited capital.

While, of course, there is no system that can be guaranteed to beat the casinos at their own games all the time,
or even in the majority of attempts, a carefully planned
and executed program of betting management can result in
numerous advantages to you, not so much against the
casino but as compared to other gamblers who are not
following any plan at all. This includes those who bet on
hunches and make random bets having no relationship to
either their previous bets or the trend of the dice.

The dice can run "hot." That is, they can be passing
many times in succession, and the gambler who bets to
pass all the time and doubles his bet after each win will

clean up handsomely if he doesn't run out of luck. I don't recommend parlaying front-line bets exclusively, for the very clear reason that when disaster strikes it is sudden and total. One lost bet following a series of wins will wipe out all of your previous gains and the amount you originally risked.

How do you know when the dice are going to start running "hot"? They can, with equal probability, run "cold." In order to cash in on such consecutive trends, whether the dice are or aren't passing, some gamblers base their betting on a repetition of the previous decision. If the dice pass eight times in succession, a gambler following this plan will have seven wins to his credit, each gain doubling the previous one if he lets all his money ride and his maximum bet is not restricted by the table limit.

Those maximum limits, by the way, can be easily circumvented by having a trusted friend help you out and do some of the betting for you.

If the dice can repeat the previous decision, they can as easily run opposite to it. Most gamblers fear such an event because to them it means that they'll lose. In my own program of management I exploit the probability that the dice will *not* repeat the previous decision as well as the probability that they will. The advantage of this will be more fully realized as we go along.

You have to parlay your *wins,* not your losses, in order to win anything at all faster than at a snail's pace. Many of the books by other authors on so-called "sure" gambling success offer the martingale system or one of its many variations, which is basically that you double your bet after each loss, and sooner or later (if you don't run out of money and luck at the same time) your luck will turn and any losses you build up will be overcome by the final big bet that you win.

Now we get into other permutations or arrangements and what they mean to us. The dictionary definition of a permutation is: "any one of all the possible arrangements in a number of objects in a series."

You may have heard of "corporations" in gambling. Two or more individual gamblers, pooling their resources or their playing efforts, are a corporation. A gambler may team up with another one in such a way that, with one agreeing to bet in a certain manner and with the other betting opposite to it, any bad luck by one will be offset, to some degree, by the good luck of the other. The hope in the operations of a corporation is that one of its members will have such good luck that it will carry the losses of the others and the corporation will show a net profit for its combined operations.

The simplest form of corporation in playing Craps is with two gamblers. One bets all the time to Pass, parlaying his bets up to a predetermined goal if several consecutive passes are made. The other, following the same mutually agreed program for the management of his betting, always bets on Don't Pass. If they're both playing at the same table they have only to wait until the dice begin following a pattern of running "hot" or "cold," then while one gambler shows moderate losses and the other has even greater gains, the corporation can be dissolved with each of its members pocketing his share of the net profit. The corporation is also effective in any other game that offers two-way betting, such as Roulette or Faro.

If the dice aren't running "hot" or "cold," then the assumption is that they're following a nearly normal pattern of results with Pass and Don't Pass decisions in about equal proportions. A corporation could be formed to try to take advantage of any pattern in which the decisions alternate, with each decision the reverse of the previous one. We could combine the two corporations just described, to make a corporation with four members in it, each one following a separate betting program from the others.

Now we get into permutations seriously because we're

less concerned with the individual decisions than in their order in a certain series.

You don't have to team up with another gambler, whom you may not trust, to enjoy the advantages of gambling in a corporation. You can be the corporation yourself.

There is something to be said in favor of your gambling as a self-contained corporation. Gamblers making side bets with one another do so to try to save money. Openly making side bets would not be tolerated in any legal gambling casino where all bets are against the house, which expects to earn an income from them. As an individual gambling as a corporation you can make side bets without the casino or its employees being aware of it. The money you put down on the gambling table is only the difference, not the sum of the otherwise individual bets by each member of the corporation.

I personally follow a combination of four basic plans for betting:

1. Bet on the front line all the time.

2. Bet on the back line all the time.

3. Start with a front-line bet, change to a back-line bet as soon as you show a net gain, then back to the front line after another net gain, and so forth.

4. Alternating bets as above, but starting with a back-line bet.

You're now covering all possible ways that the dice will go, whether the results are good, bad, or indifferent for you. Since you have your money on *any* favorable sequence that may occur, it takes some of the worries out of your gambling. If the game is being played with crooked dice, which is a possibility where Craps is not legal, your money is riding on those dice to win for you. The more crooked the dice are, the better your opportunities to win as long as the same dice remain in the game.

The individual gambler not covering all permutations is always worried that the dice will run the wrong way for him, or perhaps that they'll just go back and forth in a pass-don't-pass-don't sequence which could be disastrous if he's not betting exactly that way. Equally frustrating would be a series of favorable decisions when the player's money was not being bet on them.

In the study used in this chapter we'll begin the alternating bets at one betting unit each, and the steady front-line and back-line betting at two betting units each. Whenever a net gain is shown on any bet, the amount of the following bet is doubled.

For simplicity in following the action we'll designate the plus sign (+) to represent that the dice have passed and the minus sign (−) to show that they didn't. Let's first study the result (++++) of four consecutive passes.

	A	B	C	D		Bet	Cumulative
	Alternating, start with		Continuous		Difference	against house	net gain or loss
	+	−	+	−			
1.	W1	L1	W2	L2	0	0	none
2.	L2	L1	W4	L2	1	1 on −	lost 1
3.	L2	L1	W8	L2	3	3 on +	won 2
4.	L2	L1	W16	L2	11	11 on +	won 13
	7	4	30	8	15		

Total 49

It will be readily seen that four individual players, each separately making the bets described in Columns A, B, C, and D, would have made bets in the sum of 49 betting units. One player combining the functions of these four individuals would be risking only 15 betting units against the house. The remainder of the betting units are "hidden" ones on which the casino can't earn anything. In this example, where you get 49 betting units of action while risking only 15, the casino's earnings are reduced to less than one third of what they would otherwise be if all bets were put down on the table.

If this immediate problem is limited to a study of the permutations possible in four consecutive decisions, with the dice passing on the first one, there are only eight different arrangements for the series, and the only way they can go is one of these (reading across):

+	+	+	+
+	+	+	−
+	+	−	+
+	+	−	−
+	−	+	+
+	−	+	−
+	−	−	+
+	−	−	−

We would have the same statistical result if we started with each of the arrangements for a series of four decisions, with the dice not passing on the first one. Since it would be repetitious here to do an additional study on these just to duplicate what we are about to do anyway, we return to the eight possibilities for a series of four decisions, beginning with the dice passing on the first one, and study them in greater detail. The number of permutations in an example like this doubles with each added unit in a series. Complete studies of this type could become unwieldy if not kept down to the barest essentials.

	A	B	C	D			
	Alternating, start with		Continuous		Dif-ference	Bet against house	Cumulative net gain or loss
	+	−	+	−			
+	W1	L1	W2	L2	0	0	none
+	L2	L1	W4	L2	1	1 on −	lost 1
+	L2	L1	W8	L2	3	3 on +	won 2
+	L2	L1	W16	L2	11	11 on +	won 13
	7	4	30	8	15		

Total 49

	A	B	C	D		Bet	Cumulative
	Alternating, start with		Continuous		Dif-	against	net gain
	+	−	+	−	ference	house	or loss
+	W1	L1	W2	L2	0	0	none
+	L2	L1	W4	L2	1	1 on −	lost 1
+	L2	L1	W8	L2	3	3 on +	won 2
−	W2	W1	L16	W2	11	11 on +	lost 9
	7	4	30	8	15		

Total 49

	A	B	C	D			
+	W1	L1	W2	L2	0	0	none
+	L2	L1	W4	L2	1	1 on −	lost 1
−	W2	W1	L8	W2	3	3 on +	lost 4
+	L2	L1	W8	L2	3	3 on +	lost 1
	7	4	22	8	7		

Total 41

	A	B	C	D			
+	W1	L1	W2	L2	0	0	none
+	L2	L1	W4	L2	1	1 on −	lost 1
−	W2	W1	L8	W2	3	3 on +	lost 4
−	W2	W1	L8	W2	3	3 on +	lost 7
	7	4	22	8	7		

Total 41

	A	B	C	D			
+	W1	L1	W2	L2	0	0	none
−	W2	W1	L4	W2	1	1 on −	won 1
+	W4	L1	W4	L2	5	5 on +	won 6
+	L8	L1	W4	L2	7	7 on −	lost 1
	15	4	14	8	13		

Total 41

	A	B	C	D		Bet	Cumulative
	Alternating, start with		*Continuous*		*Dif-ference*	*against house*	*net gain or loss*
	+	−	+	−			
+	W1	L1	W2	L2	0	0	none
−	W2	W1	L4	W2	1	1 on −	won 1
+	W4	L1	W4	L2	5	5 on +	won 6
−	W8	W1	L4	W2	7	7 on −	won 13
	15	4	14	8	13		

Total 41

	A	B	C	D		Bet	Cumulative
+	W1	L1	W2	L2	0	0	none
−	W2	W1	L4	W2	1	1 on −	won 1
−	L4	W1	L4	W2	5	5 on +	lost 4
+	W4	W2	W4	L4	6	6 on +	won 2
	11	5	14	10	12		

Total 40

	A	B	C	D		Bet	Cumulative
+	W1	L1	W2	L2	0	0	none
−	W2	W1	L4	W2	1	1 on −	won 1
−	L4	W1	L4	L2	5	5 on +	lost 4
−	L4	L2	L4	W4	6	6 on +	lost 10
	11	5	14	10	12		

Total 40

The number of permutations possible with the two different items (+ and −) in a series of four, taken all at a time, are 16. We study half of these, and in this half-sample in the preceding table you'll see that out of 342 betting units of action only 94 of them were risked against the house. The immediate advantage is that, on the average, when you are getting 342 betting units of action while risking only 94, it means you risk only 27½ percent of the total, a ratio of 3.64 to 1 in your favor as compared to other gamblers who think and bet one way only and don't cover all the possible arrangements.

What we might be tempted to regard as the ideal distribution (one each of the various realignments that are possible) results in gains and losses that exactly offset each other. Before you get the mistaken idea that you have found the magic formula for nullifying the house percentage, I ought to remind you that to get that ideal distribution in any casino game except Faro your luck has to be a tiny bit better than average. The margin favoring the house is such a small one in line bets in Craps that often, in a gambling session lasting several hours, just one bet going this way or that way, out of hundreds made, will be the deciding factor in whether you win or lose during that period of time.

Go to the table just concluded two paragraphs back to study it in greater detail. You'll notice that nothing is wagered against the house in the first roll in a series because the bets in one direction balance those made in the opposite direction. In continuous play we don't sit out this one but accept the decision in the final roll of the previous series as the first of a new series and continue on from there.

In the second step, when we wager one betting unit opposite from the previous decision, we're not too concerned about whether we win or lose. It takes a minimum of two decisions to establish a trend and, if we can continue that trend for two more decisions, we'll be 13 betting units ahead by the fourth decision.

You can devise betting plans of your own if you like. You can carry each series on through more than four decisions at the risk, of course, of reducing the relative ratio of protection offered by your available capital. In stretching a series to five decisions on those occasions when you're ahead by 13 betting units after the fourth one, your risk on the fifth would normally be for 17 betting units if you're trying to make five alternating decisions in a row. It means you'll either be 4 behind or 30 ahead depending on how

that fifth decision goes. If you're ahead of the game and
feel that your good luck will continue (what gambler
doesn't, when he's winning?), this is the time to increase
your betting a little and hope for the best. Instead of 17
betting units, a bet of 20 is recommended here because it
is more conveniently associated with any betting on the
odds that you might make along with it. You can risk even
more, in moderation, depending on your ability to absorb
a loss if things go the wrong way for you.

If you *lose* four guesses in a row (we won't count the
first in a series where no money was risked against the
house) you'll lose one, then three, then three more on your
line bets and terminate that series, and from a fresh start
will lose one more as the first money bet against the house
in a new series. If you *win* four guesses in a row on those
same decisions, you'll be ahead by 30 or more betting
units on your line bets. Four correct guesses in a row win
you at least 30 betting units, four wrong guesses lose you
only 8. With a ratio of success that ought to be close to 50
percent wins on individual bets, it's worth playing Craps
when you cover all the possible arrangements and don't
stretch your luck too far on them.

Example of four consecutive wrong guesses:

Dice passed on previous decision, then the decisions
+ − − to complete the permutation + + − −,
and another Don't Pass decision in the next permutation.

Decision	Player's Bet	Result
+	no bet	
+	1 on −	lost 1
−	3 on +	lost 3
−	3 on +	lost 3
	end of permutation	
−	1 on +	lost 1
		Total: lost 8

Example of four consecutive correct guesses:

Dice passed on previous decision, then the decisions
− + − to complete the permutation + − + −.

Decision	Player's Bet	Result
+	no bet	
−	1 on −	won 1
+	5 on +	won 5
−	7 on −	won 7
	normally end of permutation, but player, being ahead, is going to press his luck on another, bigger bet	
+	17 or more on +	won 17 or more

Total: won 30 or more

You, as an individual gambler, will like this when you know that you have as good a chance of winning with the dice running about average, passing and not passing in equal proportions, as when they run continuously hot or cold. If it happens to be one of those consecutive streaks, you have no worries about whether it was due to the pure laws of chance or to some purposeful manipulation by someone working either for or against the casino. It is not likely to happen in Nevada, where the casino is supposed to be on your side, when it comes to guaranteeing the honesty of the equipment and the conduct of the game. But if you're gambling some place where there is a suspicion that crooked dice may be employed, don't be afraid of them! Those crooked dice could earn money for you.

From the table appearing earlier in this chapter it can be seen that if you lose the maximum possible in a series of four decisions on your line bets, you'll be out only 10 betting units, or 1 percent, of your capital if you're properly capitalized for 1000 times your initial betting unit. To go broke in continuous play you would have to lose heavily and steadily over a very long period of time. If you made nothing but wrong guesses on your line bets you would have to make over 426 of them in succession, an event that would require six hours, more or less, of playing at the average Crap table. If you can play for six hours without winning a single line bet, your luck is so bad you really deserve to go broke. Anyway, it shows that dividing your available capital into very small bets is a wise idea, and don't let anybody talk you out of it.

In a pure martingale system, 10 successive losing bets will set you 1023 betting units behind, enough to wipe you out, even when properly capitalized, if you are using the wrong gambling system.

The permutations and the betting described in the table are based on the gamble that four decisions will come in a certain order. The sixteen possibilities here, each of them as good as any of the others in frequency of occurrence, lull you into the delusion that with average luck, guessing right as many times as you guess wrong, you can overcome the house percentage and, in theory at least, if you have enough capital, be able to gamble indefinitely at no cost to you. If all bets were for the same amount and not doubled after showing each net gain, you actually would nullify the house percentage because all bets would be "hidden" ones in which you risked no money. You wouldn't win anything, either. In order to win any money you have to risk yours against the house, and on those bets there's a price to pay that can't be avoided, no matter how much you juggle your figures or your thinking.

Because of the house percentage that you're continually rubbing against on your line bets in Craps, you shouldn't figure to win half of them with average luck. You'll be winning about 35 to every 36 that you lose.

If you risk only the amounts shown in the table, your average bet will be $4\frac{7}{12}$, or a trifle under $4-3\frac{11}{12}$ to be exact. For statistical convenience let's say it's exactly 4 betting units.

In 288 rolls, that would require about four hours of

continuous playing at the average Crap table, you can expect to win 140 decisions and lose 144 of them, with four stand-offs. Your gambling cost—what you pay to the house for your use of its equipment—will be 16 betting units. With 10-cent betting units on a 10-cent-minimum table, that cost of $1.60 will be at the rate of almost 40 cents per hour. By making flat bets of 10 cents each you can reduce your gambling cost to less than 10 cents an hour, and if your first attempt at playing Craps is to learn the game and familiarize yourself with the way bets are handled, this is the way to get educated.

Your problem, aside from the ever-present one of avoiding going broke, is to try to overcome that small gambling cost in one way or another. Betting on the Odds gives you your best opportunity to do that. Playing Craps is real fun when you play within your means, regard it as recreation, and don't foolishly risk large sums you can't afford to lose.

The critical test of betting management in any system you may read about, including the one described in this book, is how well you can sweat it out when Lady Luck deserts you. Those unfavorable turns in your fortune burst upon you without warning. It's not rare to make ten or twelve wrong guesses in a row or to lose 70 or 80 percent of the bets you make over a fairly long period of time. When that happens, the wise player who has plenty of capital still behind him doesn't panic and try to recover his losses in one bold stroke. He then has a good chance to continue playing and once more come out ahead.

Your bets are always on futures, not on something that has already happened, and your chances of winning or losing are just as good, or just as bad, at any one time as at another. However, if you chart your progress in any gambling session, you'll see that your luck does seem to run in cycles. The frustrating part of it is that the direction and intensity of those cycles can't be predicted. If your luck is bad at the moment and you extend yourself too far and your bad luck continues, even briefly, that's the end!

The feeling of being an outsider, limited to watching the game you once participated in, is miserable. I hope it won't happen to you. It shouldn't if you know how to gamble intelligently.

CHAPTER 12

BUILDING UP YOUR FORTUNE

What you have studied thus far has emphasized playing Craps cautiously, with your main objective to avoid going broke. You did this by dividing your capital into very small parts, each betting unit being no larger than one tenth of 1 percent of your capital, and by limiting your possible losses so that with the very worst luck on any series of four decisions you won't be out more than 10 betting units, or 1 percent of your capital.

How about the long pull? Can you clean up big from a small start with your capital divided into such tiny parts?

Yes, it can be done, and it's a lot easier than you think.

Gamblers at Craps and the other casino games can take a cue from the short-term stock market speculators. In every city of any importance in the United States there is at least one stock broker with direct wires to the big security and commodity markets. Playing the stock market is a serious business to the short-term speculators, who buy and sell stocks in the hope of making a quick net profit on the transactions.

In the western part of the United States they'll get up at what seems to be an unreasonably early hour to nongamblers, for the purpose of hurrying down to their broker's at the exact time that marks the opening of the business day on the New York Stock Exchange. They want to get the figures right off the ticker tape while they're fresh. Reading the news off the teletype machines, before the radio stations and newspapers spread it to the masses, is important too. A very small change in the price or the future prospects of a stock in New York may be enough for a decision to buy or sell and cash in on a modest but certain profit.

A net gain of only 5 percent compounded 26 times (1.05^{26}) results in a product 3.56 times your original capital. If you had $10,000 to risk on the stock market and knew your securities and sources of information well enough to be able to make a 5 percent profit above your broker's commissions once every two weeks, by adding your small profits to your capital and reinvesting them, at the end of a year your $10,000 would have grown to $35,600.

The trick is to aim for the smaller but more certain profits now available, if your stock shows a slight gain (or the other way around, if you're a "Bear" instead of a "Bull"), rather than to try to make a big killing in one bold stroke. You might have to hang onto your purchases a very long time if you're holding out to double or triple your money in one buy-and-sell operation. Buying a stock at 20, for example, and selling it at $21\frac{5}{8}$ to pay your brokerage and make a small net profit may not seem like a fast way to get rich, but it's the base for many a wise stock market player's financial success.

The power of compound interest is what will put you far ahead in any financial program if you let that compound interest work for you.

In all legal gambling games except Faro you have to pay something to do your gambling. You can't use any gambling game in itself as a basis for compounding your fortune. In Craps the only bets in which your chance of winning exceeds your chance of losing are the buy bets or Odds bets against a point. At best, a bet against 4 or 10 gives odds of 1 to 2 in your favor that you'll win two thirds of such bets. That's compensated for financially by your having to risk double the amount of your expected gain. Two out of three is not a good enough frequency of winning for what we have in mind. We need something that is very strongly in your favor.

Since no situation automatically exists where your chance for a small gain exceeds your chance of losing by a very wide margin, we will have to create such a situation. This is where having sufficient capital pays off. You do this by using your capital of 1000 betting units as a base and making your short-term goal a 5 percent gain. It's very definitely in your favor that you can be 50 betting units ahead before you'll be 1000 behind.

If you make 20 5-percent gains and compound them, you will have increased your capital 2.66 times. It seems like slow progress here, but if you continue to make and compound these 5-percent gains, 50 of them will raise your capital to $11\frac{1}{2}$ times what you started with. Eighty will give you almost 50 times your original capital, and double that, or 160 5-percent gains compounded (1.05^{160}), will give you close to 2500 times your beginning investment. You could, in theory and in practice, start with only $40 and raise it up to $100,000 or more.

I've done that a number of times in my statistical studies and feel certain that anyone can do it in Nevada with real dollars instead of figures on a sheet of paper if he has the time and patience to stick to this program. If you start with more than $40, you'll need fewer of those 5-percent gains to reach your goal, and you'll be better protected against any run of bad luck that might wipe you out in the early stages of your project. For starting with 10-cent betting units, a beginning capital of not less than $100 is recommended.

Students of higher mathematics who understand and can operate a log-log duplex slide rule will find this instrument valuable in their gambling calculations. In actual play you won't be making the bets and the increases at each increment in your program in the exact amounts that your slide rule shows they should be, but with the slide-rule figures as a rough guide your goal is made very clear. Your progress toward that goal is shown even more clearly.

Let's say that from a start of $40 you have put in a full

work week (40 hours) gambling, and your capital has increased until it is now $50. To the average person that would represent a 25-percent gain and nothing else, but to a mathematician it has more significance. A 5-percent gain raised to the 4.57th power ($1.05^{4.57}$) equals 1.25.

Now $^{4.57}/_{160}$ is exactly $\frac{1}{35}$ of your long-term goal, or 2.86 percent of the distance. While uninformed observers may look on your gambling all week for a $10 gain with some doubt concerning your sanity, you can grin back at them, knowing that in 34 more weeks at the same rate of increase, compounded, you'll have in the neighborhood of $100,000.

The time required for a 5-percent increase in your capital on an infinity basis will be an average of about eight hours of continuous Crap playing. You can do it in less than a minute when luck is running with you, but as often as you start off winning you'll start off losing. Most of the time you'll recover those losses to show a net gain without much delay, but sometimes the losing streaks last for weeks and even months, in which time you won't go broke but will hover between 0 and 100 percent of your capital until you finally end up ahead. If you have the good fortune to avoid one of those extended negative sessions, your rise to riches will be a speedy one.

I've never claimed that you can't go broke. If it should happen to you in spite of your capitalization of 1000 times your initial betting unit, it will take the casino a long time to eliminate you. You'll be battling all the way, and you can be just as proud of yourself in defeat as any soldier who stuck to his assigned post and kept firing until he ran out of ammunition.

During your gambling experience, whether you play continuously or only occasionally at widely separated intervals, if you have the good luck to forge ahead in your gambling I hope you'll also have the good sense to dispose of some of your gains in such a way that the casino can't win them all back when your luck changes.

CHAPTER 13

CONCLUSIONS

The great variety of games offered in Nevada gambling requires your making a choice of which one to play, depending on the type of excitement you crave, the size of your bankroll, and what you hope to accomplish with it.

What's your gambling style?

Do you gamble conservatively, combining relative safety and economy with the recreational features of the games you play? Then you'll make small bets, play a long time, and be well pleased if you finish your gambling session with at least as much money as you started with.

Are you a plunger who risks all in a few crucial bets which will either leave you broke or more than double your money, according to how they come out?

In any case, your careful attention to certain fundamental procedures—what to do and what to avoid—will enable you to do your gambling in the manner most advantageous to you. You'll either do it at the lowest cost possible for a certain game, or you'll get the greatest return for the risks you're taking.

A brief résumé of what to watch for in each game is included in this final chapter.

CRAPS

Your best bets are the flat bets and the betting on the Odds done in connection with them. If you're really serious about playing Craps at the lowest possible cost, these are the only bets you'll make.

Place bets and buy bets are moderate in cost. Hard-way

bets and the Field are on the borderline separating the sucker bets from the others. Any one-throw bet on which the house expects to earn more than $1 for your $1 on the table through 36 throws can be considered a sucker bet. The contrast between the best bets you can make and the worst ones is brought out in Table 1 in the Appendix where the differences in the house's time-period earning rates are listed.

Any Nevada casino gives you a good break in permitting single odds for the maximum that it allows, but you get a slightly better break where you can play for double odds. When it comes to a choice between something good and the absolute best, always go for the best. Double odds are permitted in most of the casinos in Reno and on the north shore of Lake Tahoe.

It is a popular but mistaken belief held by many gamblers that a player can hope to win only when the dice are "hot" and the same shooter is throwing them a long time. This belief is furthered by some casino owners and their press agents who like to cry publicly, for its advertising value, every time they lose a sizable amount of money to front-line players.

Not so well known is that betting Don't Come on every throw of the dice can also be very profitable to players, even at times when the dice are considered "hot." It has certain advantages. It doesn't depend on any unusual performance of the dice—rather, on their normal behavior. The 7, which is feared by front-line bettors because it may mean disaster to them, is most welcome to the Don't Come bettors. There's a 7 once in every six throws, on the average, and any period in which the 7s are not spaced too far apart generally means steady progress to players who are always betting on Don't Come.

When the shooter is coming out, you would ordinarily bet on Don't Pass. Your being on the "Don't" every throw might necessitate a few changes of convenience for you and the dealer. The dealer might prefer that you put your bet in the Don't Come box even when it's the shooter's come-out, because he would be looking for all your other bets during the same roll at that spot on the layout. On the Las Vegas type of layout, you could save both yourself and the dealer a lot of extra effort if you play at the far end of the table and put the Don't Come bets on the table yourself.

After you get one or more Don't Come bets behind their respective point numbers, when the shooter throws a 7 it doesn't matter how it affects the shooter's roll. The shooter may have made a "natural" 7 and another Pass decision, and will continue throwing the dice; or the shooter may have sevened out, terminating his hand. All that's important to you is that a 7 was thrown. The steady Don't Come bettor will lose his last such bet, but at the same time it's a win for him on all his Don't Come bets already up behind their point numbers.

Laying the Odds is an essential ingredient in the success of playing this way. With only one point number involved, a sequence of throws such as 9, then 7, results in breaking even on the flat bets (you win one Don't Come bet while losing another) if you don't bet on the Odds. When you *do* lay the Odds, what you win on them is your margin of profit.

A conservative player, or one with insufficient capital for a big spread, or facing $1 minimum bets that may require heavier initial betting than he had counted on, will limit himself to only two or three points for a start. Then as he acquires more capital, if he's gaining steadily, his ability to spread out builds up with his finances until he's able to cover all six of the point numbers.

When you have all the points covered by Don't Come bets and a 7 appears, you experience a pleasure rarely felt by the average player of Craps. All losing bets are removed from the table; the other winners, if any, are paid off; then the dealer concentrates on paying you. In one multiple decision triggered by that 7 you win six Don't Come bets at one time, together with your bets on the Odds on all of them. It's the Craps equivalent of baseball's home run with the bases loaded.

The return of all the money you laid out on the table in making your bets, plus what you win from the house in 12 separate payoffs, comes your way in waves. If you make line bets of five betting units, of whatever value that unit is, and lay full double Odds against each point number, there are 124 units of your money along with 90 units you just won from the house. You have a problem—fortunately, a pleasant one. It's to pick all those chips or coins off the table so the game can go on.

If you're an average amateur gambler in Las Vegas or Reno you'll be most likely using chips valued at 10 cents or 25 cents each. In Reno where double odds prevail, at the five-chip betting level you'll win 5 chips on the line and 10 more on the Odds on each point. An experienced dealer, immediately sizing up the situation, can tell you something like: "You won a dollar-fifty times six, or nine dollars— right?" On your confirming that it is, the dealer can then simply shove all your bets back to you without treating them individually and add nine dollars as your winnings.

Where the dealer is a trainee or one without much experience or if rigid house rules specify that it be handled this way, the dealer will slowly pay off each bet separately under the watchful eye of the pit boss. This is often the case because new dealers are broken in at the Crap tables handling the lower values of chips. Regardless of the manner in which your money and your winnings are handed to you, you'll be the object of attention and, to say the least, no small amount of envy by other players at your table who lost heavily from that same 7 that was a winner for you.

The major risk you take in betting Don't Come all the time is that you may hit a stretch of quite a few throws between 7s. It can be very costly to the house against Pass and Come bettors because in accepting any bets the house is supporting the opposite decision and can't duck out of it. The squeals of the casino owners, even if they are considered in bad taste, are real ones.

You, as a player, can employ various safeguards to control and limit your losses if the dice should suddenly get "hot." One of these precautions is to limit the number of points you'll cover at one time. Then if the shooter throws points that are not covered by your Don't Come betting, you won't lose anything on them. Another is to limit the number of losses you'll sustain since the last 7 appeared. You then cease making Don't Come bets until after the appearance of another 7. For example, you have bets working against three of the point numbers and decide to sweat out the decisions on them. If your luck is bad, your bets will go down one at a time. The shooter may continue making many more throws before getting a 7, while you are happily watching all this go on without losing any more bets. This ability to take advantage of action that is favorable, while avoiding some of that which is not, is judged to be the secret of successful Don't Come betting.

Let's consider the worst that might happen to a player who is willing to cover all the point numbers but stops making Don't Come bets after three such bets affecting point numbers go down. With double odds and the points 4 or 10 involved, three losses based on five-chip line bets would cost the player 25 betting units each—a total of $7.50 if 10-cent chips are used. Then if the player is up against all six of the point numbers and the bets go down one at a time before a 7 appears to stop the damage, the loss on these would be 124 betting units, or $12.40. Summed up, a siege of the worst luck imaginable in one shooter's spread between 7s when you manage your betting this way, betting five 10-cent chips on the Don't Come and laying full double Odds, can cost you close to $20.

There is no guarantee that the same won't happen several times in succession or at closely spaced intervals, but if you have $50 or more of gambling capital at your disposal you're better able to get over these rough spots when they happen only occasionally, and your chance of survival and showing a net gain over the house remains reasonably good.

The more responsible casino owners give you valuable advice in cautioning you to divide your gambling capital into small parts to protect yourself against these temporary reverses in your luck. They don't spell out the details on how to do this. Betting on Don't Come every throw, except when there is a long spread between 7s, seems to be one of the most effective ways of insuring your survival. A total capital of only 100 times your risk on a single Don't Come bet is considered a relatively slim margin for safety, but it's a tough job indeed for the house to wipe you out. It's surprising how fast that number 7 can make money for you when it shows up at its expected frequency with clock-like regularity. The dice may be neither "hot" nor "cold," but still you can be a real threat to any gambling casino.

Don't take my word for it. Get yourself a pair of dice, pencil and paper, and do some practice. Start with a theoretical $30 in gambling capital. Make initial bets of three 10-cent chips on Don't Come every throw, lay full Odds against all points made, and if you get up to $40, increase your Don't Come bets to four chips. Then to five chips as you cross the $50 threshold, and gradually more as your progress continues. At the $75 mark in your gambling capital you can switch over to Crap tables using 25-cent chips. After going through betting at the level of three, four, five, and six chips, a capital of $200 brings you to the $2 line bet level and then you can dispense with using chips valued at less than a dollar.

You won't come out ahead every time. But if Lady Luck is on your side, during a single gambling session you can build that $30 start up to several hundred or even several thousand dollars before you suffer any serious reverses.

FARO

Faro, once played from coast to coast and the leading American gambling game of the nineteenth century, is nearly extinct. Were it not kept alive in a few Nevada casinos, learning about Faro would be an adventure into history rather than into contemporary gambling. Within the past sixty years it has been replaced by Craps as the most popular American gambling game.

Like the gamblers of recent generations, you too may not find that Faro meets your demands for a continuously exciting game. Its best feature is the cost-free gambling available on case and cat-hop bets. Coming as it does in a little over one sixth of the deals, the cat-hop offers a diversion from the ordinary ending where all three cards are of different denominations. If you figure about ten minutes for a deal, or "from soda to hock" as this term is correctly applied here, there will be a cat-hop about once in an hour's Faro playing.

"Calling the turn," or naming both the winner and the loser in the final turn if it's not a cat-hop, pays 4 to 1 and costs bettors $16\frac{2}{3}$ percent on account of this shortened payoff. Mathematically there's an exact equivalent in a one-throw bet on Any 7 in Craps. There's a throw about four times a minute in Craps compared to a final turn not a cat-hop about five times an hour in Faro. Gamblers are terribly impatient people. Waiting up to ten minutes or longer is comparative eternity to a gambler who is so impatient that he's willing to pay a heavy price for winning more than even money; hence, one good reason for the popularity of Craps. Not that betting on Any 7 is any better, but you don't have to wait as long to get some action.

There are other reasons from the player's point of view. Throughout the history of Faro, which goes back more than 500 years, the game was crooked to a degree where Faro and cheating were practically synonymous terms. The

cards, remaining permanently in the possession of the
dealer working for the house, gave unlimited opportunities
for undetected cheating. Few gambling houses failed to
take advantage of it, and when dealers were paid $100 to
$200 a week (a lot of money a hundred years ago) and
a percentage of the profits, they weren't paid that just for
pulling cards out of a dealing box. Faro as now played in
Nevada is thoroughly honest and it is the best game offered
in Nevada gambling for the average player who wants to
keep his gambling costs down to a minimum.

Since it is no longer the main source of income for the
house, you can ignore warnings in older gambling books
that a player who makes case bets only is going to find
himself very unpopular. The description that a player must
make a bet subject to possibility of a split before he can
make a case bet is not correct as it applies to Faro played
in Nevada today.

Faro today is principally an accommodation to gamblers, has some good will and advertising value for the
casino offering it, and is not expected to make a net profit
for the house. The casinos where it is played spend no
money in subsidizing travel to their gambling rooms and
can well afford to run a Faro Bank as their unique contribution to the Nevada gambling scene.

That Faro, honestly operated, cannot be a profitable
game for the casino is best proven by the fact that the
management of the casino in Monte Carlo has never in-
stalled a Faro Bank in spite of pleas from thousands of
wealthy visiting Americans during the century when Faro
attained its widest popularity in the United States. The
house percentage, whatever it could be calculated to be,
was considered to be a sham and virtually nonexistent in a
game where you can gamble absolutely free. The house's
earnings from splits would not have paid for the kerosene
or gas needed to illuminate the room. It is no wonder that
any Faro Bank in the United States was presumed to be,

ipso facto, a crooked one. It had to be if the operator expected to stay in business.

The development of the plastics industry, making possible the manufacture of nearly perfect transparent dice to replace ivory ones, was a big technological advancement that favored Craps at the expense of Faro.

Other reasons have been advanced for the decline of Faro. John Scarne, author of *Scarne on Cards* and *Scarne on Dice,* believed that Bank Craps took the business away from Faro by giving the gambler the opportunity of betting either way. Other writers claimed that Faro lost out because other casino games have a house percentage lower than 16⅔.

Faro always allowed two-way betting. It is not necessary to look to other games to find a house percentage lower than 16⅔, because Faro itself has house percentages down to zero.

The real reason for Faro's decline and replacement by Craps has not been mentioned by the few authors who have attempted to explain it. It's simply that casinos consider Craps a better money-maker than Faro, and the lower earnings or losses encountered in trying to operate an honest Faro Bank have caused most of them to abandon the game. The 16⅔ percent which the house can earn on "calling the turn" by Faro players about five times in an hour doesn't compare with the numerous betting options in Craps where the house earns that percentage or nearly as much on every throw of the dice. With an activity of about 225 throws to the hour, you can see that Craps is going to be preferred.

If you want to have the experience of playing Faro in your family without risking a loss, make a big case bet on any denomination or on high card and have your wife or husband make a similar bet coppered. One of you will win from the other. You could have tossed coins or cut a deck of cards at home, but gambling at a Faro Bank is more fun.

KENO

There's not much good that can be said about playing Keno. The few advantages to the player are ones of function and convenience, having nothing to do with the finances of the game.

If you insist on playing Keno you should look for the biggest payoffs combined with the fewest spots marked.

Tickets for less than seven spots should be avoided because parlaying line bets in Craps gives you far greater returns for similar risks. I don't recommend the ordinary eight-spot ticket, but some of the Nevada casinos offer an "8-Spot Special" that begins paying off on five spots and pays $25,000 for a perfect score on a ticket costing $1.10. This ticket can usually be bought for 55 cents also, with a top payoff of $12,500.

I consider the "8-Spot Special," if not bought in amounts exceeding $1.10 on any Keno drawing, to be the best of the tickets now available. That's not saying much for it, however, because it falls far short of what Keno players really want. Although the house percentage on it is a little greater than on the regular eight-spot ticket, it's a more exciting ticket to the player due to the increased payoffs on the two top scores.

A comparison of straight Keno tickets for ten, eleven, and twelve spots shows that Las Vegas casinos are more generous (by 2½ times) than casinos in northern Nevada for payoffs on the perfect scores.

If you're playing Keno, don't let yourself be your own worst enemy. Avoid buying any Keno ticket in an amount that may result in your winnings being crimped by the casino's aggregate payoff limit. Let's say you buy the "8-Spot Special" for $2.75. At 2½ times the $1.10 rate you should get $62,500 on the payoff for a perfect score. The casino management will pay you $25,000 with smiles and congratulations to you on your good luck, and the owners will chuckle also. They can go out shopping with $37,500 that you have unwittingly treated them to.

The question of why legal gambling casinos maintain a limit on the payoffs they'll make on a single drawing is one that ought to be answered with an explanation that makes sense, if one can be put forward. The answer usually given, that the casino can't afford to pay more, requires closer examination when you learn, for example, that the 20,000 for 1 payoff for nine hits on the "9-Spot Special" (a rate over three times the 6440 for 1 payoff on the regular nine-spot ticket) can be made as often as fifteen times the expected frequency without the game showing a mathematical loss.

The State of Nevada comes in for some criticism in allowing these limits. Any insurance or casualty company limiting its payments for losses in this manner while collecting premiums for greater contingent liabilities would be unceremoniously booted out of business in any of our fifty states by the insurance commissioner for that state.

ROULETTE

Roulette is the simplest of the casino games and also the easiest one to play. Descriptions of Roulette in gambling literature, often obtained from translations of European works, can be confusing to the Nevada gambler.

The American wheel, with its two green numbers and the practice of the casinos here to keep all of the stakes on even-money bets when a zero or double zero appears, makes even-money Roulette betting in Nevada nearly four times as expensive as in European casinos. Lately the European wheel, with only one green number, has made its debut in Nevada, but the game is still almost twice as expensive as in Europe to the even-money bettors.

Gamblers in European casinos have preferred Roulette because of its low house percentage, the manner in which the casino openly acknowledges that it is making a profit, and the complete honesty with which the game is conducted. Because the house percentage of 1.35 on even-money bets is half that on the other bets, most serious European gamblers prefer to take advantage of the lower cost and make the even-money bets. This percentage is actually lower than for line bets in Craps when you don't do any supplemental betting on the Odds.

In Nevada, where the house percentage is the same on all bets except the "House Special," you'll get more excitement from the game by making small bets on a single number for the 35 to 1 payoff. If you play that way on one of the European layouts found in Reno, then you can truly say that you're gambling for exactly the same cost that your contemporaries in Monte Carlo, Wiesbaden, or Venice are paying to make similar bets.

While Roulette as played in Nevada is not specially attractive to gamblers, because of the lower house percentages available in all of the other pit games, it does serve a useful purpose for measuring gambling costs. For example, there is a considerable difference between the lowest and highest possible house percentages in Craps, Faro, and Blackjack. You can say, unquestionably, that any bet more expensive to you than American Roulette (where the house percentage is 5.26 or more on all bets) is a sucker bet.

BLACKJACK

Blackjack is difficult to evaluate in comparison with other casino games and can best be understood separately. The house percentage cannot easily be precisely determined. The big variable factor is the skill of the individual player. In a card game with no fixed number of cards dealt to the players and to the dealer, listing all the situations that can arise, with an accurately calculated house percentage for each, would be a monumental task. A player with little or no experience at the game would be doing much more poorly at it than one who has already mastered a few of the more important fundamentals.

In your attempts to reduce the casino's earnings or convert them into a small percentage in your favor, every little stratagem that you can muster has to be used. You'll have to case the cards the best you can mentally. If remembering every denomination in the deck is a job, at least you can keep track of the number of Aces and 10-value cards used during the deal, and those still remaining in the undistributed deck.

For example, when the deck is half used up there should be two Aces and eight 10-value cards in the twenty-six remaining, with normal distribution. If there are three Aces instead of two, that extra Ace increases the possibilities of a Black Jack by 50 percent.

The value of casing the deck increases as the cards to be reckoned with become fewer. If there are only five or six cards left and you know that one is an Ace and most of the others are 10-value cards, the prospects of a gain are so much in your favor that when you know about this before the cards are dealt, you can bet more heavily than usual to press your advantage in this temporarily favorable situation.

I don't recommend Blackjack as the game for the gambler who is working on a shoestring. You need a big reserve of cash to profit from any breaks that you can find or make for yourself.

The Insurance bet, viewed independently, is practically a guaranteed money-maker for you if you make it only when there is at least a one-third probability of success. This means that (other things being equal) you're better off playing Blackjack in casinos where the Insurance bet is allowed. Selectively taking advantage of Insurance on all favorable occasions whittles a little off the casino's earnings, or, if you're breaking even or doing better otherwise, represents that much more profit to you on top of your total regular betting gains.

I found that by casing the deck, even if I sometimes wasn't able to do it with complete accuracy, I was able to play for very long periods of time and almost break even on the number of bets won and lost. Winning at least 49 percent of your bets should automatically put your Blackjack playing on a profitable basis. Consider the extra money you receive on the Black Jack bonus as the bridge that takes you over from losing to winning money. Your gains on the Insurance bets add a trifle more to your profits, and you can get still more by having your biggest bets when you have a better-than-normal chance of getting a Black Jack.

You can see that an expert player, well financed and giving his exclusive, sober attention to what he's doing, can give a gambling casino a bad time if he has any kind of luck in his favor.

Allegations of widespread cheating by Blackjack dealers in Nevada, made in recent gambling books and in the publicity resulting from the promotion of them, have to be taken with a grain of salt. Casino managers and pit bosses explain that "system" players frequently persist in these unfounded cheating claims, making them every time the player isn't winning with his system or isn't making the gains expected from it.

I often play Blackjack with my fellow employees. No money is involved. I also test various playing methods myself, dealing both the players' and the dealer's hands. In all of this playing for recreation only, there is, of course, no cheating or any motive for any. But exactly the same things that happen in Nevada casinos are observed.

The dealer will suddenly become lucky, getting counts of 20 or 21 several times in succession, to beat players' hands that are not quite as good. When the dealer has 12 and then draws a 9 to get 21 and beat your 20, then on the next play has 16 and draws a 5 to do the same thing, it is easy to jump to conclusions and think you ran into a stacked deck, or that the dealer was peeking and dealing himself seconds. Yet there is nothing here except pure chance in the way the cards are falling. Luck can go against the house as well as with it. The dealer went bust 19 times in succession in one Nevada casino, and there was nothing the house could do to prevent this losing streak. Luck is an easily recognized factor in most of the other gambling games, but in those where playing cards are used it is likely to be overlooked in explaining away a player's losses.

By all means, if you play Blackjack you should become acquainted with the various ways in which cheating *can* be done, and be on the alert for them. But if "experts" can't identify and prove any cheating taking place in Nevada casinos, you probably won't either.

I've found casino employees on occasions to be unbelievably stupid; some are so insulting that one must exercise self-restraint to keep from inflicting physical violence upon them; but in fairness to the legal gambling business, I have yet to find one who was deliberately dishonest.

Blackjack is a hard game to beat, any way you slice it, but I don't want to discourage you from playing it. The element of skill that is required brings great personal satisfaction to the players who know about it and are making serious efforts to improve their playing abilities.

Now that you're acquainted with some of the details for putting forth your best possible performance in gambling, a look at gambling as a whole, without reference to your individual playing, is in order.

What purpose does Nevada gambling serve? How does it compare with legal gambling elsewhere? What are its future prospects?

Legalized gambling is a political experiment in dealing with a social (or moral) problem, on the assumption that if you can't stop the activity, the next best thing is to legalize it, control it, tax it, and spend some of the money thus obtained for the public good.

Nevada does that quite well. The revenues from gambling licenses and taxes relieve its citizens of the necessity of paying state income taxes.

The Nevada experiment with legalized casino-type gambling could not be carried out in any of our more densely populated areas. Most of the gamblers come from other states. This has a favorable impact on the tourist trade. Outside money flows into Nevada.

The mere legitimacy of gambling is no guarantee that a player can't be cheated, or that he's being protected from schemes so highly favorable to the casino that they could more accurately be called legalized robbery than gambling. The same type of casino activity found in Nevada also flourished in Cuba before the Castro revolution put a stop to it, but Havana had become infamous for the rigged equipment and crooked dealers employed there.

Nevada even allows the notorious "football parlay" type of bets on sports events to be made openly. These bets cover football, baseball, basketball, or whatever happens to be the popular sport at the moment. Players buck a house percentage of over 88 percent on a nine-game baseball parlay. In addition, they're so willing to be fleeced that they gladly pay an added 10 percent federal tax on their bets. As long as the suckers don't squeal too loudly, the game is profitable to the operators, and the state and federal governments extract some tax revenue from it, almost anything seems to go.

State control over gambling, doing a very good job with the personnel and means at its disposal, is centered in a Gaming Commission and a Gaming Control Board. The competitive nature of Nevada gambling means that the business to a large extent polices itself, but the necessity for a superior authority is evident. The gambling business has never been without its incompetents and black sheep, in Nevada as well as anywhere else, and weeding them out and preventing them from getting in is a full-time job for those entrusted with this responsibility. Obviously, this has to be done by officials who are not personally involved in the ownership or operation of any of the casinos.

You should regard Nevada gambling as a fluid matter, subject to change or even abolition at any time. Nevada has gone through several of these off-and-on cycles in its brief history, and in 1909, when outside gambling interests attempted to take over control of its Legislature, the answer to that was to make gambling illegal so there would be no incentive for out-of-state racketeers to muscle in on what seemed like a sure thing, operated within the law. It was not until 1931 that gambling was once more legalized in Nevada.

Gambling is legal in at least half of the states, and in six of them the state's revenue derived from gambling taxes exceeds that earned by Nevada. Legal gambling elsewhere refers primarily to pari-mutuel betting on horse and dog racing.

Why American gamblers respect the Nevada casino games, in spite of serious shortcomings in some of them, is easy to understand. Nevada is the only state in which you can play Craps, Faro, Roulette, Keno, and Blackjack legally, and you have an unprecedented degree of honesty in the conduct of the games and supervision over them that isn't available to gamblers in states where these games are illegal.

APPENDIX

1. Craps—average time-period earning rates by the casino, and other useful information

Type of Bet	Advertised Payoff	House's Advantage Percent	House's Advantage Fraction	For 36 throws with $1 on the table (est'd time 9.6 min.) the house earns[a]	For 252 throws with $1 on the table (est'd time 1 hr. 7.2 min.) the house earns[a]	Remarks[e] (all applicable to 252 throws)
Flat Bets:						
Pass or Come	even money	1.414	1/72[b]	$ .14¾	$ 1.00	
Don't Pass or Don't Come	even money	1.402[a]				
Place Bets:						
On 6 or 8	7 to 6	1¹⁷⁄₃₃	1/66	.16⅔	1.16⅔	On full place bet of $6, house earns $7
On 5 or 9	7 to 5	4	1/25	.40	2.80	On full place bet of $5, house earns $14
On 4 or 10	9 to 5	6⅔	1/15	.60	4.20	On full place bet of $5, house earns $21
Field (2, 3, 4, 9, 10, 11, 12)*	even money on 3, 4, 9, 10, 11; double on 2; triple on 12.	2⅔	1/36	1.00	7.00	On $32 spread on all point numbers, off on come-outs, house earns $30
Hard-Way 6 or Hard-Way 8	9 to 1	9¹⁄₁₁	1/11	1.00	7.00	
Hard-Way 4 or Hard-Way 10	7 to 1	11⅙	1/9	1.00	7.00	
Big 6 or Big 8	even money	9¹⁄₁₁	1/11	1.00	7.00	

Bet	Payoff				Minimum bet $3; house earns $84
Field (2, 3, 4, 9, 10, 11, 12)*	even money on 3, 4, 9, 10, 11; double on 2 and 12.	5%	$1/18$	2.00	14.00
		11%	$1/6$	4.00	28.00
Any 7*	13 to 3°	11½%	$1/6$	4.00	28.00
Any Craps (2, 3, or 12)*					
5 or 9*	7 to 1	11½%	$1/6$	4.00	28.00
3 or 11*	7 to 1	11½%	$1/6$	4.00	28.00
2 or 12*	15 to 1	11½%	$1/6$	4.00	28.00
2 or 12*	30 to 1	13%	$1/7.2$	5.00	35.00
3 or 11*	29 to 1	16⅔%	$1/6$	6.00	42.00
2 or 12*	14 to 1	16⅔%	$1/6$	6.00	42.00
Any 7*	4 to 1	16⅔%	$1/6$	6.00	42.00
Under 7*	even money	16⅔%	$1/6$	6.00	42.00
Over 7*	even money	16⅔%	$1/6$	6.00	42.00
Horn (2, 3, 11, or 12)*	if it pays 15 to 4 on any winning number	20%	$1/4.8$	7.50	Minimum bet $2; house earns $105 — 52.50

(*) single-throw bet
(a) omitting stand-off on the barred number
(b) all flat bets as a group
(c) this payoff rate not marked on any layout; you have to ask for it
(d) based on 225 throws per hour and average of 3.5 throws to a decision on line bets.
(e) these figures are for play at $1-minimum tables

2. Keno Probabilities

The percentage of probabilities in each stratum of performance from no hit to the maximum number of hits possible for the ticket, expressed to eight decimal places or to five significant digits if extended further.

HITS	1-SPOT TICKET	2-SPOT TICKET	3-SPOT TICKET
3			1.38753651
2		6.01265823	13.87536514
1	25.00	37.97468354	43.08666018
0	75.00	56.01265823	41.65043817
Total	100.00	100.00	100.00

HITS	4-SPOT TICKET	5-SPOT TICKET	6-SPOT TICKET
6			.01289849
5		.06449247	.30956385
4	.30633923	1.20923380	2.85379178
3	4.32478914	8.39350523	12.98195475
2	21.26354658	27.04573907	30.83214254
1	43.27318251	40.56860861	36.34947331
0	30.83214254	22.71842082	16.66017527
Total	100.00	100.00	100.00

HITS	7-SPOT TICKET	8-SPOT TICKET	9-SPOT TICKET
9			.000072427
8		.00043457	.00325925
7	.00244026	.01604552	.05916784
6	.07320767	.23667137	.57195579
5	.86385048	1.83025856	3.26014806
4	5.21909667	8.15037015	11.41051821
3	17.49932414	21.47862252	24.61092163
2	32.66540507	32.81456217	31.64261352
1	31.51925051	26.64641139	22.06655943
0	12.15742520	8.82662377	6.37478384
Total	100.00	100.00	100.00

HITS	10-SPOT TICKET	11-SPOT TICKET	12-SPOT TICKET
12			.00000020909
11		.0000016030	.000016727
10	.000011221	.00010580	.00054280
9	.00061206	.00283736	.00954010
8	.01354194	.04114169	.10195984
7	.16111431	.36078097	.70273859
6	1.14793946	2.02037345	3.22088520
5	5.14276877	7.40803597	9.93873147
4	14.73188971	17.85865813	20.57628002
3	26.74023678	27.83849650	27.97298200
2	29.52567811	26.80744108	23.77703470
1	17.95713756	14.39136315	11.37657162
0	4.57907008	3.27076434	2.32271671
Total	100.00	100.00	100.00

HITS	13-SPOT TICKET	14-SPOT TICKET	15-SPOT TICKET
15			.00000000023364
14		.0000000025700	.000000035046
13	.000000024599	.00000030840	.0000020677
12	.0000023984	.000014784	.000064960
11	.000094337	.00038110	.00123425
10	.00200623	.00597377	.01520596
9	.02598976	.06082380	.12671626
8	.21831401	.41816365	.73314406
7	1.23151495	1.98512854	2.98897196
6	4.75012902	6.57573830	8.63480787
5	12.58784190	15.19726186	17.61500806
4	22.72804787	24.22063609	25.02131827
3	27.27365745	25.90442362	24.04009011
2	20.66186170	17.62939941	14.79390160
1	8.88097564	6.85191232	5.22792012
0	1.63956473	1.15014243	.80161442
Total	100.00	100.00	100.00

3. Keno Payoff Ratios and House Percentages

Sixty-one distinct basic price and payoff structures for straight Keno tickets are shown here. These are, in most cases, the minimum price at which each particular type of ticket can be purchased. The 50-cent rate is sometimes obtainable in fractions of that price—such as 15 cents, 20 cents, 25 cents, and so forth—all having the same payoff ratios to the price of the ticket.

All tickets can be purchased in multiples of the basic unit, and many of them are advertised that way. Thus, the 50-cent ticket will be repeated at double the payoff figure for it under "Play $1," and at 10 times that amount under "Play $5."

Whenever the maximum payoff on any ticket is restricted by the casino's aggregate payoff limit to players in each game, the house percentage goes up due to the shortened payoff ratio.

	1-SPOT TICKET 50¢ RATE		2-SPOT TICKET 50¢ RATE		3-SPOT TICKET 50¢ RATE	
HITS	PAYS	RATIO	PAYS	RATIO	PAYS	RATIO
1	$1.60	3.20				
2			$6.50	13.00	$ .50	1.00
3					23.50	47.00
	House Percentage 20.00		House Percentage 21.84		House Percentage 20.91	

	4-SPOT TICKET 50¢ RATE		5-SPOT TICKET 50¢ RATE		5-SPOT TICKET 50¢ RATE	
HITS	PAYS	RATIO	PAYS	RATIO	PAYS	RATIO
2	$ .50	1.00				
3	2.50	5.00	$ 1.50	3.00	$ 1.50	3.00
4	59.00	118.00	13.00	26.00	13.00	26.00
5			180.00	360.00	166.00	332.00
	House Percentage 20.96		House Percentage 20.16		House Percentage 21.97	

	5-SPOT TICKET 55¢ RATE		6-SPOT TICKET 50¢ RATE		6-SPOT TICKET 55¢ RATE	
HITS	PAYS	RATIO	PAYS	RATIO	PAYS	RATIO
3	$ 1.50	$2.72\frac{8}{11}$	$ .50	1.00	$ .50	$.90\frac{10}{11}$
4	13.00	$23.63\frac{7}{11}$	2.80	5.60	2.80	$5.09\frac{1}{11}$
5	225.00	$409.09\frac{1}{11}$	55.00	110.00	62.50	$113.63\frac{7}{11}$
6			620.00	1,240.00	740.00	$1,345.45\frac{5}{11}$
	House Percentage 22.14		House Percentage 20.99		House Percentage 21.14	

	7-SPOT TICKET 50¢ RATE		7-SPOT TICKET 50¢ RATE		7-SPOT TICKET 50¢ RATE	
HITS	PAYS	RATIO	PAYS	RATIO	PAYS	RATIO
0	$ .50	1.00			$ .50	1.00
1					.15	.30
2					.15	.30
3	.20	.40	$ .50	1.00	.20	.40
4	1.65	3.30	2.50	5.00	1.00	2.00
5	12.10	24.20	15.00	30.00	8.00	16.00
6	136.00	272.00	50.00	100.00	88.00	176.00
7	750.00	1,500.00	750.00	1,500.00	750.00	1,500.00
	House Percentage 19.14		House Percentage 19.51		House Percentage 20.78	

	8-SPOT TICKET 50¢ RATE		8-SPOT TICKET 50¢ RATE		8-SPOT TICKET 50¢ RATE	
HITS	PAYS	RATIO	PAYS	RATIO	PAYS	RATIO
3	$ .05	.10				
4	.75	1.50	$ .80	1.60	$ .75	1.50
5	7.20	14.40	7.20	14.40	7.20	14.40
6	53.90	107.80	53.90	107.80	54.00	108.00
7	402.50	805.00	402.50	805.00	400.00	800.00
8	1,920.00	3,840.00	1,920.00	3,840.00	2,000.00	4,000.00
	House Percentage 19.17		House Percentage 20.51		House Percentage 21.28	

	8-SPOT TICKET 55¢ RATE		8-SPOT TICKET 65¢ RATE		8-SPOT TICKET $1.00 RATE	
HITS	PAYS	RATIO	PAYS	RATIO	PAYS	RATIO
0			$ .65	1.00		
3					$ .10	.10
4					1.55	1.55
5	$ 5.00	9.09 1/11	6.00	9.23 1/13	14.40	14.40
6	45.00	81.81 9/11	86.00	132.30 10/13	107.80	107.80
7	1,100.00	2,000.00	500.00	769.23 1/13	805.00	805.00
8	12,500.00	22,727.27 3/11	3,500.00	5,384.61 7/13	3,840.00	3,840.00
	House Percentage 22.03		House Percentage 28.13		House Percentage 18.76	

	8-SPOT TICKET $1.30 RATE		8-SPOT TICKET $2.20 RATE		8-SPOT TICKET $2.60 RATE	
HITS	PAYS	RATIO	PAYS	RATIO	PAYS	RATIO
3	$ .10	.07 9/13			$ .25	.09 8/13
4	1.95	1.50	$ 1.20	.54 6/11	3.95	1.51 12/13
5	18.55	14.26 12/13	20.00	9.09 1/11	37.15	14.28 11/13
6	129.35	99.50	181.00	82.27 3/11	258.70	99.50
7	1,125.00	865.38 9/13	4,425.00	2,011.36 4/11	2,250.00	865.38 9/13
8	3,750.00	2,884.61 7/13	25,000.00	11,363.63 7/11	7,500.00	2,884.61 7/13
	House Percentage 21.70		House Percentage 22.23		House Percentage 21.10	

	8-SPOT TICKET $2.60 RATE		8-SPOT TICKET $3.20 RATE		8-SPOT TICKET $6.00 RATE	
HITS	PAYS	RATIO	PAYS	RATIO	PAYS	RATIO
3	$ .25	.09 8/13	$ .35	.10 15/16		
4	3.95	1.51 12/13	5.00	1.56 1/4	$ 6.00	1.00
5	37.15	14.28 11/13	46.45	14.51 9/16	90.00	15.00
6	258.70	99.50	323.40	101.06 1/4	500.00	83.33 1/3
7	2,000.00	769.23 1/13	2,769.25	865.39 1/16	8,400.00	1,300.00
8	7,500.00	2,884.61 7/13	9,230.75	2,884.60 15/16	25,000.00	4,166.66 2/3
	House Percentage 22.26		House Percentage 19.29		House Percentage 21.73	

	8-SPOT TICKET $12.80 RATE		9-SPOT TICKET 35¢ RATE		9-SPOT TICKET 40¢ RATE	
HITS	PAYS	RATIO	PAYS	RATIO	PAYS	RATIO
3	$ 1.30	.10 5/32				
4	19.90	1.55 15/32	$ .15	.42 6/7		
5	185.80	14.51 9/16	1.80	5.14 2/7	$ 1.80	4.50
6	1,293.50	101.05 15/32	17.80	50.85 5/7	17.80	44.50
7	10,000.00	781.25	110.70	316.28 4/7	110.70	276.75
8	25,000.00	1,953.12 1/2	1,000.00	2,857.14 2/7	2,600.00	6,500.00
9			2,250.00	6,428.57 1/7	6,000.00	15,000.00
	House Percentage 21.28		House Percentage 20.76		House Percentage 21.23	

9-SPOT TICKET 40¢ RATE

HITS	PAYS	RATIO
5	$ 1.20	3.00
6	14.40	36.00
7	196.00	490.00
8	2,160.00	5,400.00
9	8,788.00	21,970.00

House Percentage 21.45

9-SPOT TICKET 45¢ RATE

HITS	PAYS	RATIO
5	$ 1.35	3.00
6	16.00	$35.55\tfrac{5}{9}$
7	220.00	$488.88\tfrac{8}{9}$
8	2,430.00	5,400.00
9	9,000.00	20,000.00

House Percentage 21.91

9-SPOT TICKET 45¢ RATE

HITS	PAYS	RATIO
5	$ 1.50	$3.33\tfrac{1}{3}$
6	20.00	$44.44\tfrac{4}{9}$
7	165.00	$366.66\tfrac{2}{3}$
8	2,500.00	$5,555.55\tfrac{5}{9}$
9	10,500.00	$23,333.33\tfrac{1}{3}$

House Percentage 22.02

9-SPOT TICKET 50¢ RATE

HITS	PAYS	RATIO
4	$ .20	.40
5	2.60	5.20
6	26.00	52.00
7	160.00	320.00
8	1,430.00	2,860.00
9	3,220.00	6,440.00

House Percentage 20.02

9-SPOT TICKET 50¢ RATE

HITS	PAYS	RATIO
4	$ .20	.40
5	2.55	5.10
6	25.40	50.80
7	158.10	316.20
8	1,428.60	2,857.20
9	3,214.30	6,428.60

House Percentage 21.27

9-SPOT TICKET 50¢ RATE

HITS	PAYS	RATIO
4	$ .20	.40
5	2.55	5.10
6	25.40	50.80
7	158.10	316.20
8	1,428.55	2,857.10
9	3,214.20	6,428.40

House Percentage 21.27

9-SPOT TICKET 55¢ RATE

HITS	PAYS	RATIO
0		
5	$ 2.00	$3.63\tfrac{7}{11}$
6	27.00	$49.09\tfrac{1}{11}$
7	175.00	$318.18\tfrac{2}{11}$
8	3,000.00	$5,454.54\tfrac{6}{11}$
9	11,000.00	20,000.00

House Percentage 23.56

9-SPOT TICKET 65¢ RATE

HITS	PAYS	RATIO
0	$ .65	1.00
5	2.00	$3.07\tfrac{7}{13}$
6	25.00	$38.46\tfrac{2}{13}$
7	259.00	$398.46\tfrac{2}{13}$
8	1,800.00	$2,769.23\tfrac{1}{13}$
9	5,000.00	$7,692.30\tfrac{10}{13}$

House Percentage 28.28

9-SPOT TICKET $1.25 RATE

HITS	PAYS	RATIO
0		
5	$ 5.00	4.00
6	60.00	48.00
7	400.00	320.00
8	5,000.00	4,000.00
9	10,000.00	8,000.00

House Percentage 26.96

10-SPOT TICKET 50¢ RATE

HITS	PAYS	RATIO
0		
5	$ 1.00	2.00
6	9.00	18.00
7	90.00	180.00
8	650.00	1,300.00
9	1,300.00	2,600.00
10	12,500.00	25,000.00

House Percentage 20.56

10-SPOT TICKET 50¢ RATE

HITS	PAYS	RATIO
0		
5	$ 1.00	2.00
6	9.00	18.00
7	90.00	180.00
8	650.00	1,300.00
9	1,300.00	2,600.00
10	5,000.00	10,000.00

House Percentage 20.74

10-SPOT TICKET 65¢ RATE

HITS	PAYS	RATIO
0	$ 1.00	$1.53\tfrac{11}{13}$
5		
6	10.00	$15.38\tfrac{6}{13}$
7	100.00	$153.84\tfrac{8}{13}$
8	1,000.00	$1,538.46\tfrac{2}{13}$
9	2,000.00	$3,076.92\tfrac{4}{13}$
10	10,000.00	$15,384.61\tfrac{7}{13}$

House Percentage 27.62

11-SPOT TICKET 50¢ RATE

HITS	PAYS	RATIO
5	$ .50	1.00
6	5.00	10.00
7	38.00	76.00
8	242.00	484.00
9	768.00	1,536.00
10	2,318.00	4,636.00
11	12,500.00	25,000.00

House Percentage 20.18

11-SPOT TICKET 50¢ RATE

HITS	PAYS	RATIO
5	$ .50	1.00
6	5.00	10.00
7	38.00	76.00
8	240.00	480.00
9	800.00	1,600.00
10	2,000.00	4,000.00
11	5,000.00	10,000.00

House Percentage 20.24

11-SPOT TICKET 55¢ RATE

HITS	PAYS	RATIO
5	$ .60	$1.09\tfrac{1}{11}$
6	5.10	$9.27\tfrac{3}{11}$
7	42.30	$76.90\tfrac{10}{11}$
8	267.00	$485.45\tfrac{5}{11}$
9	845.00	$1,536.36\tfrac{4}{11}$
10	1,800.00	$3,272.72\tfrac{8}{11}$
11	5,500.00	10,000.00

House Percentage 20.74

	11-SPOT TICKET 65¢ RATE		12-SPOT TICKET 40¢ RATE		12-SPOT TICKET 50¢ RATE	
HITS	PAYS	RATIO	PAYS	RATIO	PAYS	RATIO
0	$ 1.00	1.53 11/13				
5			$ .25	.62 1/2	$ .30	.60
6	5.00	7.69 3/13	2.25	5.62 1/2	2.60	5.20
7	40.00	61.53 11/13	14.95	37.37 1/2	18.70	37.40
8	372.00	572.30 10/13	85.20	213.00	106.00	212.00
9	1,000.00	1,538.46 2/13	299.25	748.12 1/2	374.00	748.00
10	2,000.00	3,076.92 4/13	720.25	1,800.62 1/2	1,026.00	2,052.00
11	12,500.00	19,230.76 12/13	1,533.25	3,833.12 1/2	3,166.00	6,332.00
12			4,000.00	10,000.00	12,500.00	25,000.00
	House Percentage 28.96		House Percentage 19.51		House Percentage 20.03	

	12-SPOT TICKET 50¢ RATE		12-SPOT TICKET 60¢ RATE		12-SPOT TICKET 65¢ RATE	
HITS	PAYS	RATIO	PAYS	RATIO	PAYS	RATIO
0			$ 2.00	3.33 1/3	$ 1.00	1.53 11/13
5	$ .30	.60				
6	2.60	5.20	3.00	5.00	2.00	3.07 9/13
7	18.70	37.40	22.00	36.66 2/3	20.00	30.76 12/13
8	106.50	213.00	128.00	213.33 1/3	176.00	270.76 12/13
9	374.00	748.00	450.00	750.00	500.00	769.23 1/13
10	912.80	1,825.60	1,000.00	1,666.66 2/3	1,100.00	1,692.30 10/13
11	1,916.60	3,833.20	2,000.00	3,333.33 1/3	2,200.00	3,384.61 7/13
12	5,000.00	10,000.00	10,000.00	16,666.66 2/3	15,000.00	23,076.92 4/13
	House Percentage 20.10		House Percentage 20.52		House Percentage 28.97	

	13-SPOT TICKET 50¢ RATE		13-SPOT TICKET 50¢ RATE		13-SPOT TICKET 65¢ RATE	
HITS	PAYS	RATIO	PAYS	RATIO	PAYS	RATIO
0					$ 1.00	1.53 11/13
7	$ 9.00	18.00	$ 9.00	18.00	10.00	15.38 6/13
8	53.00	106.00	53.00	106.00	63.00	96.92 4/13
9	460.00	920.00	460.00	920.00	500.00	769.23 1/13
10	2,200.00	4,400.00	1,100.00	2,200.00	2,500.00	3,846.15 5/13
11	4,240.00	8,480.00	2,240.00	4,480.00	4,500.00	6,923.07 9/13
12	6,000.00	12,000.00	6,000.00	12,000.00	10,000.00	15,384.61 7/13
13	8,000.00	16,000.00	12,500.00	25,000.00	20,000.00	30,769.23 1/13
	House Percentage 21.12		House Percentage 25.92		House Percentage 28.97	

	13-SPOT TICKET 95¢ RATE		14-SPOT TICKET 50¢ RATE		14-SPOT TICKET 50¢ RATE	
HITS	PAYS	RATIO	PAYS	RATIO	PAYS	RATIO
5	$ .35	.36 16/19				
6	2.85	3.00				
7	17.70	18.63 6/19	$ 5.00	10.00	$ 5.00	10.00
8	100.10	105.35 15/19	28.50	57.00	28.00	56.00
9	360.10	379.05 5/19	197.00	394.00	179.00	358.00
10	950.30	1,000.31 11/19	700.00	1,400.00	402.00	804.00
11	2,035.00	2,142.10 10/19	4,000.00	8,000.00	2,000.00	4,000.00
12	4,110.00	4,326.31 11/19	9,000.00	18,000.00	4,500.00	9,000.00
13	9,540.00	10,042.10 10/19	18,500.00	37,000.00	9,200.00	18,400.00
14			25,000.00	50,000.00	25,000.00	50,000.00
	House Percentage 23.09		House Percentage 20.66		House Percentage 28.49	

HITS	14-SPOT TICKET 65¢ RATE PAYS	RATIO	14-SPOT TICKET $1.25 RATE PAYS	RATIO	14-SPOT TICKET $5.00 RATE PAYS	RATIO
0	$ 1.00	1.53 11/13				
5			$ .30	.24	$ 1.25	.25
6			2.30	1.84	9.25	1.85
7	5.00	7.69 3/13	13.40	10.72	53.50	10.70
8	35.00	53.84 6/13	70.65	56.52	282.65	56.53
9	200.00	307.69 3/13	253.25	186.60	1,013.05	202.61
10	1,480.00	2,276.92 4/13	694.00	555.20	2,775.90	555.18
11	5,000.00	7,692.30 10/13	1,552.40	1,241.92	6,209.50	1,241.90
12	10,000.00	15,384.61 7/13	3,060.00	2,448.00	12,240.00	2,448.00
13	20,000.00	30,769.23 1/13	5,900.00	4,720.00	23,600.00	4,720.00
14	25,000.00	38,461.53 11/13	13,000.00	10,400.00	25,000.00	5,000.00
	House Percentage 24.96		House Percentage 23.27		House Percentage 23.00	

HITS	15-SPOT TICKET 50¢ RATE PAYS	RATIO	15-SPOT TICKET 50¢ RATE PAYS	RATIO	15-SPOT TICKET 65¢ RATE PAYS	RATIO
0					$ 1.00	1.53 11/13
7	$ 4.00	8.00	$ 3.90	7.80	4.00	6.15 5/13
8	14.00	28.00	14.00	28.00	15.00	23.07 9/13
9	82.00	164.00	82.00	164.00	100.00	153.84 6/13
10	315.00	630.00	315.00	630.00	400.00	615.38 6/13
11	1,300.00	2,600.00	1,300.00	2,600.00	2,400.00	3,692.30 10/13
12	6,000.00	12,000.00	6,000.00	12,000.00	10,000.00	15,384.61 7/13
13	14,000.00	28,000.00	14,000.00	28,000.00	20,000.00	30,769.23 1/13
14	25,000.00	50,000.00	25,000.00	50,000.00	25,000.00	38,461.53 11/13
15	25,000.00	50,000.00	25,000.00	50,000.00	25,000.00	38,461.53 11/13
	House Percentage 21.15		House Percentage 21.74		House Percentage 28.98	

HITS	15-SPOT TICKET $1.50 RATE PAYS	RATIO
5	$ .25	.16 2/3
6	1.80	1.20
7	9.80	6.53 1/3
8	48.85	32.56 2/3
9	172.35	114.90
10	480.00	360.00
11	1,107.45	738.30
12	2,225.00	1,483.33 1/3
13	4,130.00	2,753.33 1/3
14	7,700.00	5,133.33 1/3
15	16,000.00	10,666.66 2/3
	House Percentage 22.86	

Note: A payoff of $10,000 for 15 hits (6666.66⅔ payoff ratio), shown on some tickets, does not materially affect the house percentage. So little money proportionately is paid on the perfect score that the house percentage would have to be projected to six decimal places before a difference would show.

4. Glossary

ace	The score on a die with one spot uppermost.
ace-deuce	A score of 1–2 for a total of 3 with a pair of dice. (Craps)
American wheel	The Roulette wheel with 38 compartments numbered from 1 to 36, and 0 and 00.
back line	The boxes, marked Don't Pass and Don't Come, where flat bets that the dice won't pass (won't win) are made. (Craps)
back line, betting on the	Betting that the dice won't pass (won't win). (Craps)
Bank Craps	Craps as played in legal gambling casinos, where all bets are against the house, which is banking the games.
barred number	Either the 2 or the 12, as marked on the Crap-table layout, on which Don't Pass or Don't Come bets are a stand-off if the barred number is thrown on the come-out.
Big 6	A bet, made in the box marked Big 6, that 6 will be thrown before 7. (Craps)
Big 8	A bet, made in the box marked Big 8, that 8 will be thrown before 7. (Craps)
black, bet on	An even-money bet on the 18 black numbers on the Roulette layout.
Black Jack	Two cards with a total value of 21—an Ace coupled with a 10, Jack, Queen, or King. (Blackjack)
Blackjack	The card game of "21."
box	The marked section on the Crap-table layout reserved for the bet described in it.
box bet	A one-throw bet equally divided among the numbers 2, 3, 11, and 12, usually paying off at the rate for the winning number on the amount covering that number. (Craps)
box cars	A score of 6–6 for a total of 12 with a pair of dice. (Craps)

box man   The employee who handles called bets that are not marked on the Crap-table layout.

broke   Same as *bust*.

burned card   The unused top card in a single-deck Blackjack deal.

bust   A count of over 21 in Blackjack.

buy bet   A place bet made at correct odds, on which the player pays a commission of 5 percent of the short end of the bet for making it. Can be made either for or against any selected point number. (Craps)

calling the turn   Naming in advance both the winner and the loser in the final turn and making a bet to that effect. (Faro)

case   The abacus-type counting board on which a record is kept of the cards used in the deal and whether they won or lost. (Faro)

case bet   An even-money Faro bet on a denomination when three are gone and only one remains in the dealing box, and there is no advantage to the house.

case keeper   The employee who operates the case during the Faro game.

casing the deck   Counting down the cards.

cat-hop   The situation when two cards of the same denomination are among the last three in the dealing box. (Faro)

cat-hop bet   Calling the turn in the cat-hop situation, on the gamble that the case card will either fall as the winner, the loser, or the hock.

cold   In Craps when the dice are losing (not passing) much more frequently than passing, they are said to be running "cold."

column play   A bet on the 12 numbers in the long column headed by 1, 2, or 3 on the Roulette layout, paying 2 to 1.

Come bet   A flat bet that the dice will pass, made at any time in the roll after the come-out. (Craps)

come out (v)   To start a new roll by the shooter. (Craps) *come-out* (*n*)   The first throw in a roll. On Come or Don't Come bets, the first throw after the bet is made. (Craps)

copper (*v*)   To put a copper on a bet. (Faro)

copper (*n*)   A small six-sided chip put on a bet to signify that the bet is on the loser. (Faro)

count-down   A mental count of the cards and some of the denominations that are important to a player, those that remain unused in the deck at any time during the deal.

counting down   Starting with the count for a full deck and subtracting the cards of various denominations and suits as they are dealt or played.

crap   A score of 2, 3, or 12 with a pair of dice. (Craps)

crap out   To throw a crap (2, 3, or 12) on the come-out. Less correctly, a decision that the dice didn't pass. (Craps)

Craps, Any   A one-throw bet on the numbers 2, 3, and 12.

Craps Eleven   A one-throw bet equally divided between Any Craps and 11.

croupier   The employee who pays off and collects bets in Roulette.

deal   The action in which all of the cards in the deck have been handled, necessitating reshuffling or replacement of the deck. (Faro and Blackjack)

dealer   The employee who is dealing the cards (Faro and Blackjack) or who pays off and collects bets in Craps.

dealing box   The box or cage from which the cards are dealt in Faro.

decision   The final throw in a roll in Craps, resulting in a win, loss, or stand-off on the shooter's line bet.

Don't Come   A flat bet that the dice won't pass, made at any time in the roll after the come-out. (Craps)

Don't Pass   A flat bet that the dice won't pass, made immediately before the come-out by the shooter. (Craps)

double down   To increase a bet in Blackjack and take one hit on the hand being played.

down	A term signifying that a one-throw bet has been lost; also applies to hard-way bets and other bets when there is a losing decision on them. (Craps)
dozens, bet on	A bet on the first, second, or third dozen numbers on the Roulette layout (1 to 12, 13 to 24, or 25 to 36), paying 2 to 1.
drag down	To remove any revocable bet from the gambling table.
European wheel	The Roulette wheel with 37 compartments, numbered from 1 to 36, and 0.
even, bet on	An even-money bet on the 18 even numbers on the Roulette layout.
even-money bet	Any bet that pays off exactly as much as the bettor risks. In Roulette, any of the "outside bets" covering 18 numbers: red, black, odd, even, high, or low.
Faro Bank	The layout for the Faro game, also the gambling house that banks the game.
Faro dealer	The employee who deals the cards in Faro.
Field	A one-throw bet covering the numbers 2, 3, 4, 9, 10, 11, and 12, paying off as marked on the layout. (Craps)
flat bet	Any bet made at even money.
flat money	The money risked on a flat bet. In place bets in Craps, that portion of the bet on which the house pays even money.
front line	The boxes marked Pass or Come where bets that the dice will pass (win) are made. (Craps)
front line, betting on the	Betting that the dice will pass (win). (Craps)
gag bet	Same as *hard-way bet.* (Craps)
hand	In Blackjack, the two or more cards being played by each individual player and the dealer. In Craps, the total number of rolls that a shooter has before passing the dice to the next shooter.
hand, long	A hand consisting of a large number of rolls. (Craps)

hard 17 (or
any other
count)
A Blackjack count without using an Ace, or when any Ace in the hand counts as 1.

hard-way bet
A bet that a certain even-numbered score will be made with both dice identically spotted before that score appears the "easy way," with dice not identically spotted, and before a 7 appears. (Craps)

heel-and-toe
bet
A heeled bet on one card to win and another to lose. (Faro)

heeled bet
A combination bet on two denominations, made with the bottom chip resting on or pointing to one card, and the other chips in a stack resting on an edge of the bottom chip and leaning toward the other card in the combination. (Faro)

high, bet on
An even-money bet on the 18 high numbers (19 to 36) on the Roulette layout.

high-card bet
A bet on the highest-ranking denomination in the turn to be the winner, or the loser if coppered. (Faro)

high-low bet
A one-throw bet equally divided between 2 and 12. (Craps)

hit
To deal another card to a player's Blackjack hand at the player's request.

hock
The last card in the dealing box. (Faro)

hole
The marked section on the Blackjack-table layout where the player makes his bets.

hole card
The card that the dealer has dealt face down to himself or to any player in the natural distribution of two cards to each. (Blackjack)

hop
A single throw of the dice. (Craps)

Horn bet
Same as the box bet. A one-throw bet equally divided among the numbers 2, 3, 11, and 12, usually paying off at the rate for the winning number on the amount covering that number. (Craps)

hot
In Craps, when the dice are passing (winning) much more frequently than not passing, they are said to be running "hot."

house per-centage	The house's advantage in any gambling game or betting option when expressed as a percentage of the money risked by the player.
House Special bet	A bet on the first five numbers (0, 00, 1, 2, and 3) on the American Roulette layout, paying 6 to 1.
Insurance bet	The player's bet that the dealer will get a Black Jack, made when the dealer's showing card is an Ace.
laying the Odds	Making a bet on the Odds when your bet is that the point won't be made. You risk more than what you expect to win. (Craps)
long end of bet	The larger amount risked in any bet that is not at even money.
lookout	The Faro employee who supervises the game and sees that all bets are correctly made and paid off and that the case is correctly kept.
loser	The first card out of the dealing box in a turn, which falls in the stack alongside the dealing box. (Faro)
low, bet on	An even-money bet on the 18 low numbers (1 to 18) on the Roulette layout.
martingale	A system of betting in which the amount of the bet is doubled after a loss.
miss	Failure of the dice to pass: a crap thrown on the come-out, or 7 appearing before the point. (Craps)
natural	A 7 or 11 thrown on the come-out. (Craps) The first two cards dealt to a hand. (Blackjack)
odds	Probability that a gambler will lose his bet, compared to his chance of winning it. The odds are always expressed in whole numbers, the first figure of the ratio being the gambler's probability of losing.
Odds, betting on the	A supplementary bet allowed to Crap players with flat bets, in which additional money may be wagered at correct odds that the point will or won't be made.
odds, correct	A payoff that corresponds with the exact probability of the risk involved, in which there is no advantage to the house.

odds-on	Odds at less than even money, where the gambler risks more than he expects to win.
off (*bets off*)	Temporary removal of any revocable bet from the action at the Crap table by reversing the puck or putting a "Bet Off" marker on the bet.
outside bet	A bet not made on the numbered part of the Roulette layout: specifically, the even-money bets and the bets on columns and dozens.
parlay	A system of betting in which the gambler, after a win, risks the whole stake on the next bet.
Pass	A throw or series of throws resulting in the dice winning (passing) either by the shooter throwing a natural on the come-out or by making his point in the action that follows. (Craps)
pit boss	A supervisory employee who has jurisdiction over the pit games.
pit games	The gambling-casino games (Blackjack, Craps, and Roulette) under the immediate supervision of a pit boss.
place bet	A bet on a selected point number that the point will appear before a 7. (Craps)
point	Any of the numbers 4, 5, 6, 8, 9, or 10; or one of those six numbers thrown on the come-out. (Craps)
point bet	Same as *place bet*.
press	To increase a bet following a win on it.
proposition	A bet, usually referring to the one-throw and hard-way bets. (Craps)
puck	The large round marker used to identify the point in the action at the Crap table.
quarter play	A bet on any four numbers making a square on the Roulette layout, paying 8 to 1.
rank	The denomination of the playing card. (Faro)
red, bet on	An even-money bet on the 18 red numbers on the Roulette layout.
revocable bet	Any bet which may be withdrawn after it has been made, before a decision is reached on it.
roll	One complete sequence of throws on which the shooter either wins or loses. (Craps)

seven out   To throw a 7 before repeating a point. This
                     results in termination of the shooter's hand.
                     (Craps)

shill   An employee of the casino playing with the
                     house's money for the purpose of simulating
                     activity at a gambling game not patronized at
                     the time by cash customers.

shoe   The box or cage from which the cards are dealt.
                     (Baccarat, Chemin-de-Fer, and in some casinos,
                     Blackjack, when multiple decks are used)

shooter   The player who is throwing the dice. (Craps)

short end of   The lesser amount risked in any bet that is not
   bet   at even money.

showing card   The card that the dealer has dealt face up to
                     himself. (Blackjack)

side bets   Bets made directly between players, usually in
                     Open Craps. They are not permitted in Bank
                     Craps, where all bets are against the house.

single-throw   A bet that is decided (won or lost) on one
   bet   throw of the dice. (Craps)

snake eyes   A score of 1–1 for a total of 2 with a pair of
                     dice. (Craps)

soda   The exposed top card in the deck when the full
                     deck is placed in the dealing box. (Faro)

soda to hock   The complete deal, from top to bottom of the
                     deck. (Faro)

soft 17 (or   A Blackjack count which includes an Ace val-
   any other   ued as 11.
   count)

split (n)   Two cards of the same denomination in a turn.
                     (Faro)

split (v)   To break up a pair of the same denomination or
                     value and play each as the first card in a sepa-
                     rate hand. (Blackjack)

split play   A bet on any two adjacent numbers on the Rou-
                     lette layout, paying 17 to 1.

stand   To play a Blackjack hand as is without asking
                     for a hit (another card).

stand-off   A tie or draw; a bet which nobody wins. Also
                     applies to any gambling game where one bet

	that wins is offset by another that loses a similar amount.
stick man	The employee who uses a stick to return the dice to the shooter after each throw. (Craps)
stiff	A Blackjack count (hard 12 or higher) in which a hit can result in a possible bust.
straight play	A bet on a single number on the Roulette layout, paying 35 to 1.
street play	A bet covering three numbers across on the Roulette layout, paying 11 to 1.
take one down for double	To increase a bet in Blackjack and take one hit on the hand being played.
taking the Odds	Making a bet on the Odds when your bet is that the point will be made. You risk less than what you expect to win. (Craps)
throw	One toss of the dice upon the table. (Craps)
tiger	The traditional symbol for the Faro game. "Bucking the Tiger" means playing Faro.
tourneur	In European gambling casinos, the employee who spins the wheel and throws the ball in Roulette.
turn	Each pair of cards worked in the Faro game, consisting of the loser (which falls alongside the dealing box) and the winner (which remains on top of the deck in the dealing box).
up	Signifying that a bet is working. "You're up," when said by the dealer and confirmed by the player, means that a bet previously made is being continued or repeated. (Craps)
vigorish	A slang expression for the house's margin of gross profit in any gambling game or betting option.
whipsawed	Losing two bets at one time, particularly in a heel-and-toe bet when both cards appear in reverse order to the direction of the bet. (Faro)
winner	The card remaining on top of the deck in the dealing box on each turn. (Faro)

DOLPHIN BOOKS

OF GENERAL INTEREST

ALEXANDER, HENRY   The Story of Our Language, C383
BAGEHOT, WALTER   The English Constitution, C241
BESTON, HENRY   Herbs and the Earth, C271
BIERCE, AMBROSE   The Devil's Dictionary, C225
BULFINCH, THOMAS   The Age of Fable, C132
DARWIN, CHARLES   The Origin of Species, C172
FORTUNE, EDITORS OF   The Executive Life, C69
FOWKE, EDITH, & GLAZER, JOE   Songs of Work and Freedom, C240
HOFFMAN, JOSEPH G.   The Life and Death of Cells, C156
LEONARD, RICHARD ANTHONY   The Stream of Music, C358
MYERS, C. KILMER   Light the Dark Streets, C193
PIKE, JAMES A.   The Next Day, C272
ROOSEVELT, ELEANOR   You Learn by Living, C407
VERISSIMO, ERICO   Mexico, C327
WEYER, EDWARD, JR.   Primitive Peoples Today, C200

DOLPHIN REFERENCE SERIES

AMERICAN GEOLOGICAL INSTITUTE   Dictionary of Geological Terms, C360
CARTMELL, VAN H.   Plot Outlines of 100 Famous Plays, C400
COPELAND, LEWIS, ed.   Popular Quotations for All Uses, C201
FROST, S. E., JR.   Basic Teachings of the Great Philosophers, C398
FULLER, EDMUND   2500 Anecdotes for All Occasions, C191
GOODMAN, ROLAND A.   Plot Outlines of 100 Famous Novels, C309
KAHN, GILBERT, & MULKERNE, DONALD J. D.   How Do You Spell It?, C453
MALLERY, RICHARD D.   Grammar, Rhetoric and Composition for Home Study, C381
MULKERNE, DONALD J. D., & KAHN, GILBERT   How Do You Spell It?, C453
REITHER, JOSEPH   World History at a Glance (Revised), C406
SARGENT, R. STANSFELD, & STAFFORD, KENNETH R.   Basic Teachings of the Great Psychologists, C397
SIMON, HENRY W.   100 Great Operas and Their Stories, C100
WITHERSPOON, ALEXANDER M.   Common Errors in English and How to Avoid Them, C382

DOLPHIN BOOKS

PERSONAL AND PRACTICAL GUIDES

DOLPHIN BOOKS

COOKBOOKS

MARRIAGE AND THE FAMILY

DOLPHIN GUIDES

DOLPHIN BOOKS

AMERICAN FICTION

DOLPHIN BOOKS

BRITISH FICTION

CONTINENTAL AND OTHER FICTION

DOLPHIN BOOKS

POETRY AND DRAMA

BROWNING, ELIZABETH BARRETT Sonnets from the Portuguese and Other Poems, C209
CERF, BENNETT, & CARTMELL, VAN H., eds. 24 Favorite One-Act Plays, C423
FITZGERALD, EDWARD, trans. The Rubáiyát of Omar Khayyám, C28
FRANKENBERG, LLOYD, ed. Invitation to Poetry, C24
GILBERT, W. S. *The Mikado* and Five Other Savoy Operas, C158
MARQUIS, DON archy and mehitabel, C26
OMAR KHAYYAM The Rubáiyát of Omar Khayyám, trans. FitzGerald, C28
SHAKESPEARE, WILLIAM Shakespeare's Sonnets, C33
TENNYSON, ALFRED, LORD Idylls of the King, C165
WHITMAN, WALT Leaves of Grass (1855), C3
WILDE, OSCAR The Plays of Oscar Wilde, C137

ESSAYS AND LETTERS

BACON, FRANCIS Essays of Francis Bacon, C67
CREVECOEUR, J. H. ST. JOHN Letters from an American Farmer, C164
DOUGLAS, WILLIAM O. An Almanac of Liberty, C115
LAMB, CHARLES The Essays of Elia *and* The Last Essays of Elia, C6